Food for Champions

Also by Ned Bayrd

The Thin Game:
Dieting Scams and Dieting Sense

Food for Champions

How to Eat to Win

Ned Bayrd and Chris Quilter

HOUGHTON MIFFLIN COMPANY · BOSTON
1982

Library of Congress Cataloging in Publication Data

Bayrd, Ned.
Food for champions.

Includes index.
1. Athletes—Nutrition.   I. Quilter, Chris.
II. Title.
TX361.A8B38   613.2′024796   81-20285
ISBN 0-395-31820-3   AACR2

Printed in the United States of America

V 10 9 8 7 6 5 4 3 2 1

For M.R.

Contents

Contents

Preface

SPORTS HAVE BEEN an essential part of every age and culture. Minoan Crete glorified its bull leapers and imperial Rome its gladiators, for whom colosseums were built in every outpost of the empire. The ancient Persians played polo, and the Aztecs played pelote, the forerunner of soccer, rugby, and football.

Alongside the arts, sports must be ranked as one of humankind's greatest inspirations. And as outlets for innate aggressions, sports are the closest we've ever come to a "moral equivalent of war." More importantly, sports provide pleasure. Through them we get in touch with, and revel in, our physical nature, hone our skills, test our limits, challenge ourselves and our opponents, and learn how to compete and cooperate. These are the joys of sports.

Every sport has its recognized champions. But in a very real sense, if we love sports, we can all be champions — even if we come in dead last every time. If, when the game is over, we can honestly echo Saint Paul — "I have fought the good fight. I have finished the course. I have kept the faith." — then we have won, no matter what the final score. We've done our best.

Food for Champions has been written for all athletes who want to do their nutritional best. It separates the facts from the fictions, and it presents the latest nutritional findings of sports science, an exciting new discipline that is analyzing every aspect of performance to help athletes do their best. If you'd like to learn an easy, personalized, scientific way to eat to win, this book is for you.

Acknowledgments

FOOD FOR CHAMPIONS draws upon the research of countless experts in nutrition, medicine, and sports science. We are indebted to all these explorers for their findings on diet, health, and performance.

We are especially grateful to the following individuals, each of whom brought a special perspective to our manuscript: Edwin Bayrd, M.D., Durling Professor of Medicine at Mayo Medical School, and Clifford Gastineau, M.D., consultant in nutrition and Endicott Professor of Medicine at Mayo Medical School; Dr. John Serfass, Director of Sports Medicine, University of Minnesota; James Walden, M.A. Nutrition, St. Luke's Hospital; and Alan Kristal, Dr. P.H., Columbia University School of Public Health, Division of Epidemiology.

We would also like to salute Ellen Joseph, our editor at Houghton Mifflin, for her support, enthusiasm, and patience; and our copy editor, Peggy Burlet, for her many helpful suggestions.

PART ONE

The Parameters of Nutrition

1

Eat to Win

Many of the dietary superstitions of primitive tribes are based on the ideas that certain foods — in particular the meat of certain animals — endow the consumer with the qualities of strength, endurance and courage with which his prey was identified. Trainers and coaches have inherited something of this theory and have applied it to athletes under their tutelage.

LAURENCE E. MOREHOUSE
and AUGUSTUS T. MILLER
Physiology of Exercise

Nutrition may be defined as the science of food as it relates to health and performance.

GEORGE M. BRIGGS and
DORIS HOWES CALLOWAY
Nutrition and Physical Fitness

YOU ARE WHAT you eat. Who said it first? Solomon? Socrates? Shakespeare, perhaps? Or was it Tiny Tim? It hardly matters. Like most familiar sayings, we've heard this one so often that we've come to accept it unquestioningly, as part of our common lore, our tribal wisdom. We rarely give any real thought to what such catch-phrases actually mean. This is what makes them dangerous. Live according to the wisdom that he who hesitates is lost, for instance, and you might not live to regret that you didn't think to look before you leap. Are we really what we eat? The question deserves some serious thought — and some straight answers.

3

Back in the days when we lived in caves and camps, we were all athletes. The game was survival. It must have seemed an unequal contest then. We were slower and weaker than most of the animals we hunted — and all of the animals that hunted us. But we were also smarter. We taught ourselves to swing clubs, heave rocks, and throw flint-tipped spears with accuracy. We loped for hours in pursuit of game, and escaped what was pursuing us by leaping over rushing streams or into still lakes.

Most importantly, we learned the survival value of team play. One of us was no match for a woolly mammoth; ten of us, working together, were. By necessity, we all tried out for the team. Those who couldn't make it — the weak, the slow, the clumsy — were cut. Permanently.

For those of us who did make the team, life was, nevertheless, brutal and short. We envied the attributes of stronger, fleeter, nimbler creatures; so we ate them. Supposedly, the heart of the lion would endow us with courage; the liver of the deer would give speed; the shoulder muscles of the bull would grant strength. Hindsight, always 20/20, tells us that cunning, not courage, dethroned the king of beasts. Stealth, not swiftness, snared the deer. Teamwork, not strength, penned the bull. But because we prospered on such a diet, the notion that you are what you eat prospered too. The dubious became dogma.

As savagery gave way to civilization, it ceased to be necessary for all of us to be athletes. In a surer and more complex world, the weak, the slow, and the clumsy could prosper alongside the strong, the fleet, and the agile. Other abilities mattered more. But few of us stopped admiring those primitive survival skills, and many continued to practice them. They no longer had much practical application, so we gave them ritual significance. We created sports.

The rituals of athletic competition have largely replaced the necessities of hunting and hand-to-hand combat. We have evolved — from the lions and the cavemen, to the lions and the Christians, to the Lions and the Cowboys. Today, we swing clubs with graphite or hardwood shafts. We heave "rocks" made of iron or pigskin. Our javelin lacks the flint tip, and our marathons are run on urban blacktop as often as on rural savanna. We leap over "streams" of sand or sawdust, and we leap into chlorinated pools. The circumstances have changed, but the basic challenges — and the basic satisfactions — are the same. Victory equals survival. Because it does, athletes still seek a competitive edge — in training, in equipment, and in diet.

The relationship between diet and performance is known to have preoccupied the ancient Olympians and their gymnasts, or physician-trainers. Meat was considered such an important component of the athlete's diet that fillets of beef were awarded the victors along with their laurel wreaths. The Greek physician Galen, who served the gladiatorial school in his native Pergamum in the second century A.D., likewise recommended a diet rich in animal protein for his charges.

Eighteen centuries after Galen, we are still searching for foods that are genuinely *ergogenic* — those that increase the capacity for bodily or mental labor, especially by eliminating fatigue symptoms. Like medieval alchemists, we look for ergogenic substances that will transform leaden bodies into gold-medal winners. We believe — as implicitly if not as literally as did our prehistoric ancestors, the first Olympians, and Galen's gladiators — that we are what we eat. By eating differently, then, we expect to be able to eat our way to greater strength, swiftness, agility, and endurance and, in the process, to health, happiness, and long life. The question, of course, is how.

In the absence of hard evidence, we turn to various sources for inspiration. Deer liver isn't on the modern menu. But the long muscles of the bull are, and we eat them in abundance in the tradition of the earliest athletes. In addition, we adhere to the old adage that imitation is the sincerest form of flattery by emulating modern Olympians' lifestyles, training habits, and diets. Of course, no one tells us that for lionheartedness we should rely on tablets of dessicated lion heart. But we are encouraged to eat the breakfast food that Bruce Jenner claims to eat. And we're hardly discouraged from hoping that it will make us champions too.

The results of such sincere flattery are hard to detect — until we've discovered that what sits well in the champ's stomach doesn't necessarily sit at all in ours. Well, we tell ourselves, there are always other champs and other supposedly sure-fire ergogenic regimens. So we continue to contribute to the millions of dollars spent annually on pills, powders, and products of questionable nutritional value and no ergogenic advantage. Meanwhile, study after study

5

has shown that most of us follow a day-to-day diet that is both too high in calories and out of balance. Ironically, our society is remarkably concerned with nutrition and fitness, yet surprisingly ignorant about both. Are you? Take the following test, and you'll be able to gauge how much you actually know about the impact of diet on performance.

> You've reached your tennis club's semifinals. It's hot and humid, and you're sweating profusely. You won the first set easily and lost the second by only a hair. Before the final set, you down a glass of Gatorade to replace the potassium, magnesium, sodium, glucose, and water you've sweated off. You watch in amazement as your opponent drinks more than a quart of water. In the last set, you are wiped off the court. Why?

ANSWER: Both you and your opponent had an overwhelming need for one nutrient — water — and your opponent took in more of this ideal athletic drink. In addition, drinks with sugar can dramatically reduce the rate at which water leaves your stomach and enters your system, where it's needed. (You'll learn about water, the neglected nutrient, in chapter 8.) You do lose potassium, magnesium, sodium, and glucose, as well as water, when you sweat. But unless you've been playing all out for at least two hours, you have plenty of glucose (the form of sugar used by the body) in reserve. As for the trace minerals known as electrolytes, the worst time to replace them is during exercise. You'll get all you need at your next meal.

> You and your best friend have been neck-and-neck competitors in shorter races. Now you're both going to run your first marathon. Your friend forgoes your traditional prerace meal, a Big Mac and a milk shake, because he has been carbohydrate-loading. Later in the day, you stagger across the finish line in 3.08:24. You wait ten minutes for your friend — and another ten. What went wrong?

ANSWER: An amateur, especially a first-timer, is much better off sticking to a familiar diet routine even if it's less than ideal nutritionally. The wisest choice of pregame nutrients will not contribute as much to a sense of well-being as a tried-and-true approach. And strict carbohydrate loading is arduous, complex, and controversial. In inexperienced hands, it can backfire badly. (Chapter 6 suggests a modified approach that eliminates the drawbacks.)

After a solid career in high-school football, you win an athletic scholarship to the college of your choice. The freshman coach sees that you're on the light side for college ball and recommends a summer weight-training program. At your hometown gym, the instructor says that protein supplements will help you add muscle, not just pounds. But for maximum weight gain, he says, anabolic steroids are the answer. Which should you choose?

ANSWER: Neither. You've heard that you need extra protein to build extra muscle. But you've heard wrong. Chances are, you could probably build as much muscle, if not more, with half the protein you're getting already (see chapter 5). Steroids (discussed in chapter 11) are as common as candy in big-league football, bodybuilding, and other strength sports. They are also some of the most dangerous drugs that athletes, particularly growing athletes, can take. You have all summer and your freshman year to gain the weight you need to make varsity (and you won't have to wonder why your sex drive has taken a sabbatical).

You and two friends stop before the last leg of a four-hour cross-country ski outing. It's very cold and dry; so you haven't been sweating, even though you've been skiing steadily and hard. One friend has a bag of trail mix (mostly nuts and raisins). The other has a thermos of hot broth. Your jug of tea with honey is stone cold. Which is best for a quick energy boost?

ANSWER: The tea. That it's cold doesn't matter much. In your stomach, it and the broth will soon reach the same temperature. Your body does need the water in either, because, even though you haven't been sweating, water has been evaporating into the dry air through your pores and lungs. But after the several hours of hard work, your body has also used up its most readily available supplies of energy. You can replace a bit with the sugar that's in the honey and the raisins. However, under the stress of exercise and cold weather, the body slows or stops digestion so that it can concentrate on maintaining its temperature and endurance. Under these conditions, the dissolved sugar in the tea is much more easily absorbed; you would be home before the sugar in the raisins was digested and absorbed.

You're a wrestler, bantamweight boxer, or promising member of a ballet company, and you have a weight problem. You have to lose

7

seven pounds fast. Your options are the sweatbox, fasting, diuretics (drugs that increase urine output and thereby result in the loss of body water), a high-protein diet such as the Scarsdale diet, and diet pills. Pick one.

ANSWER: Pick none if you want to perform well. Anyone who tries to lose that much weight quickly will lose strength and stamina too. Of course, any of these approaches might work for you. But unnecessary sweating is a waste of energy. The "euphoria" of fasting is nothing but lightheadedness. Diuretics can dangerously dehydrate. High protein diets sap energy by displacing carbohydrates, the high-performance fuel. Prescription diet pills containing amphetamines are no longer legal in many states. They do curb the appetite, but they also distort perception by affecting the central nervous system. If you are having so much trouble maintaining or reaching your desired weight, change your weight class, and concentrate on building strength and stamina. Also read chapter 17 to find out how to lose weight.

* * *

If you were able to separate all the nutritional facts from the fictions, pass this book along to a friend. If you weren't, continue reading. No matter what your age, sex, sport, or skill, the following chapters will enable you to acquire a competitive edge, one that comes from understanding what optimal nutrition is all about.

The information is based on the findings of sports science, which has emerged from the studies of medicine, social science, and nutrition. In universities and medical centers from coast to coast, skilled professionals have been systematically studying the diet-performance connection. Using cross-cultural studies and statistics, historical surveys, and their own observations of athletes in the laboratory, in training, and in competition, they have gathered conclusive evidence. There *are* ergogenic foods that can be eaten to improve performance. This book will tell you what they are, how they work, and how you can make the most effective use of them, starting with the one thing that other self-help nutrition books always leave out.

2

The Limits of Nutrition

Conditioning and athletic skill rank far and away as the most important factors in successful athletic performance. Nutrition can only assist to the extent that the diet is adequate in essential nutrients.

THE AMERICAN MEDICAL ASSOCIATION

POPULAR NUTRITION BOOKS never seem to mention the one thing we most need to know: nutrition cannot work miracles. Protein won't build muscles in the absence of exercise. Vitamins won't enhance vitality, no matter how many are taken. Cocaine won't sharpen skills, nor will amphetamines ("speed") improve timing. By knowing what nutrition cannot do, you can better appreciate what it can do.

Eating is an elemental and essential human activity. As a result, it has always been given social, psychological, and spiritual meanings that aren't directly connected with nutrition. These meanings can be as life enhancing as the special satisfaction that comes from feeding family and friends. But they can also interfere with good nutrition by exaggerating or obscuring its importance. Fads, myths, and superstitions that impart to any food or any way of eating a magical, medicinal, or therapeutic power are asking nutrition to keep promises it has never made. Food is, first and foremost, fuel. What is remarkable is not how well we run on "high-test," but how well we run without it.

Take Mildred, for example. She's the woman who offers the

9

glowing testimonial for the tonic you take — or is it the multi-vitamin you swallow with your breakfast juice? Or the Hi-Pro N-R-G bar you depend on when your energy sags? Mildred is everywhere these days, it seems, especially between the covers of the latest nutritional best-sellers. For most of her life, Mildred was a mess. Chronic ill health. No energy. She ate too much, smoked too much, and, frankly, she drank too much as well. Then Mildred discovered the remarkable Regimen X. In no time at all, she was a new person: vital, alive, and, to her husband's delight, the woman she was always meant to be.

We've all read about near-miracles like Mildred's many times in many books, magazines, and ads. Yet, skeptics or converts, we've overlooked the obvious: Mildred and the others had been abusing their bodies for years. What is remarkable is not the regimens they swear by, but the fact that their bodies forgave them.

The body is tough and resilient. It can adapt to a wide range of diets and function normally. It can also take an amazing amount of nutritional abuse before it loses its ability to snap back or breaks down entirely. Many athletes eat "wrong" yet perform well. They may even become better athletes. All that can be said is that in the long run, the odds are against them.

Individual health may be mysterious, but nothing is mysterious about actuarial tables, the insurance company's equivalent of the tout's racetrack odds. According to the tables, diet does matter. For every centenarian who proudly announces that his secret for a long, healthy life has been a pint of whiskey and three packs of cigarettes a day, hundreds of thousands are long dead from cirrhosis of the liver, lung cancer, and other cardiovascular and pulmonary diseases. The question worth answering is not, Does diet matter? but How much does it matter?

Putting nutrition in perspective and developing realistic nutritional attitudes may be the most important changes we can make concerning diet and its role in athletic performance. By doing so, we free ourselves from needless anxiety, anxiety that can compromise our chances of victory far faster than the wrong choice of breakfast cereal. Total abstinence from Twinkies, Yoo-Hoo drinks, Ruffles, and Sara Lee will not necessarily improve our performance, nor will occasional overindulgence hurt it. Nutritional extremism, even the most admirable kind, works only for those who are by nature extremists. Everyone else needs to strike a realistic balance, in nutritional attitudes as well as in eating patterns. Such moderation may not seem demanding enough — until you have tried it.

Enough Is Enough: The Scandal of Hypernutrition

Hypernutrition is a fancy name for a condition that is common among athletes. It results from their belief, widely promoted by the food-supplement industry, that more is better: more protein builds more muscle, more vitamins give you more vitality, more minerals provide more endurance, and so forth. With all the hype, it's hard to believe that, when it comes to nutrition, enough is enough, more is almost never better, and sometimes more is distinctly worse. Athletes, with too little information but with an understandable eagerness to gain that competitive edge, can have a hard time sorting the facts from the bunko.

You might not get much help from your favorite sports magazine. We reviewed a number of these magazines — not the feature articles but the ads. The running magazines received highest marks. One issue carried fourteen major ads for running shoes, a full-page ad for Gatorade, and a smaller one for a line of vitamin supplements masquerading as stress reducers, joint lubricators, and endurance boosters. Every runner needs running shoes, but no runner needs Gatorade specifically or vitamin supplements generally. Nevertheless, this advertising balance is commendable compared with that in bodybuilding magazines. In a recent issue of the leading publication, there were twelve major ads for equipment and fourteen for an awesome number of nutritional supplements, not one of which is necessary during even the most intensive weight training.

The very location of these ads, in publications regarded as sports Bibles, lends credibility to their claims. The claims are always the same, just as they are always carefully hedged to meet Truth in Advertising standards: Aren't you worried that your diet lacks a certain vital ergogenic something? Why take a chance on compromising your performance when you can take our product? Champion X swears by it: "Yup, it sure worked for me!" Not surprisingly, then, American athletes are seduced into spending their hard-earned money on totally unnecessary foods and supplements.

Advertisers want us to think of our diets in terms of deficiencies, when in fact the vitamins, minerals, protein, and sugar they are pushing are already overabundant in the typical American diet. Encouraging anyone, especially athletes, to supplement the over-supply is a scandal. They may call it insurance, but it's really a rip-off.

There's a limit to how much our bodies can comfortably handle, as we discover every time we overtrain. The same is equally true when we overload our bodies with nutrients. We force them to work overtime to digest and eliminate the surplus. These processes take energy. Not a great deal, to be sure, and our bodies *can* meet the challenge. But why ask them to? And why not use that energy to increase our skill, stamina, and strength?

If you find yourself confused by the conflicting claims of various diet plans and dietary supplements, remember two basic rules:

1. If you can detect a profit motive, be suspicious of all claims made for the ergogenic powers of a product. The manufacturers of vitamin tablets have manufactured the market for vitamin tablets, on which Americans squander an estimated five hundred million dollars every year. Remember that the ad you read, no matter how convincing it sounds, has been written to sell the product.

2. Personal testimonials are no substitute for scientific proof. Athletes who attribute their success to a special diet or a new dietary supplement may sound convinced. They may even be convinced. But conviction alone is not enough. It can turn you into a believer, but it cannot make you a winner. Keep in mind that professional athletes, no matter how sincere they sound, are paid to endorse products.

The solution to hypernutrition is not to ban the ads that promote it. The solution is to ignore the ads. Armed with the facts, which you'll find in the upcoming chapters, you can do this in complete confidence. You probably do need to modify your diet, but you don't need a single pill, powder, or potion.

Diet and Performance

Nutrition may matter more to Olympic-class runners than to Sunday golfers. But it should be viewed the same way by both groups.

The Athlete's Nutritional Advantage

If you are an active athlete, you need extra calories just to maintain your weight. Unless you get these calories from junk foods that are only sugar and fat, the extra food you eat will supply all the additional nutrients you require. This includes the so-called stress vitamins, minerals, and protein that all those ads say you're supposedly losing during strenuous exercise. (How large is this loss? The ads never say, because the actual amounts are embarrassingly small.) Just as importantly, exercise improves digestion, the process that breaks food down so that the nutrients can be absorbed. It also improves circulation, which carries nutrients to every part of the body. Finally, by stimulating the excretory system, it makes the elimination of wastes through the kidneys, intestines, lungs, and skin more efficient. These are the reasons why, as an active athlete eating no better than your sedentary friends, you enjoy a nutritional advantage.

Runners who take their dietary regimen so seriously that they credit it for victory and blame it for defeat are as off the mark as golfers who think that their diets have nothing to do with their performance. Not even the most enthusiastic athletes should overrate optimal nutrition. The best eating habits in the world are no substitute for practice, which sharpens skills, and exercise, which alone builds muscle. Likewise, not even the most casual athletes should dismiss the necessity of sensible eating habits, which can affect their health and longevity, as well as their game.

Nutrition is only one component of athletic performance, and in no sport is it the paramount one. Tennis champ Chris Evert Lloyd is a vegetarian, and marathoner Bill Rodgers loves junk food. It is impossible to predict how these world-class athletes would fare if they switched diets. But the relationship of diet and performance can be placed in similar perspectives for them, and for us.

The Dimensions of Competition

Every athletic activity includes three basic dimensions: physical, mental, and environmental. Each is composed of many factors, which together determine the outcome of any sports event. The physical dimension comprises health, endurance, strength, and skill; the mental dimension, attitude, alertness, and intelligence; and the environmental, weather, setting, and equipment. The easiest way to understand the role of nutrition in athletic performance is to examine each of these factors in turn.

Health. Nutrition plays an important role in health, which is really the absence of sickness. So do lifestyle, personality, and genes. Some of us may have concrete constitutions, but the rest of us endanger our health with the poor eating habits that are typical of our society. Well-nourished people enjoy better health and longer lives because they are more resistant to disease, including heart disease, hypertension, and cancer. Being well nourished, however, does not require hypernutrition. And health shouldn't be confused with fitness. Chronic poor health quickly undermines fitness, but the basically fit person can feel bad yet perform well.

Endurance. The key component of fitness is endurance. In endurance training, the heart and lungs become more efficient, delivering more oxygen to working muscles and disposing of more heat and waste products. We *train* for endurance. We *eat* for energy to fuel that training. Because endurance training is energy-intensive, your diet can make a real difference.

Strength. Popeye notwithstanding, strength comes from exercise, not spinach, and strength is maintained and increased through continued exercise. A burst of strength or speed, however, is not necessarily a sign of fitness. We can't have stamina without fitness, but we can have strength and speed without stamina. Though less energy-intensive than endurance training, "muscling up" does require energy. So nutrition matters.

Skill. Whatever special ability a sport requires, it comes to the same thing: some of us have it, some never will, and the rest must practice to improve. A diet that helps to maintain ideal weight and energy may help by removing the handicap that any overweight athlete carries onto the field. However, the key to skill is not nutrition. It's practice.

Attitude. Call it motivation, grit, team spirit, the will to win, the killer instinct, or simply self-confidence, it's essential to a winning performance. Nutrition doesn't affect attitude — unless we're guilt-ridden when we eat "wrong" or convinced that we can't win unless we eat "right."

Alertness. Sleep and attitude are far more important to alertness than is nutrition. Diet matters if it denies us the basic energy we need to perform. Then we'll begin tired or tire faster along the way. The various substances, legal and illegal, that can be taken to increase alertness won't improve performance. In fact, they'll often have the opposite effect (see chapter 11).

Intelligence. There's some evidence that those who eat "right" from birth have a "nutritional" edge on intelligence tests. Yet there's no evidence that so-called brain foods do more for the brain than for any other part of the body. Most of us could probably eat more wisely than we do now, but doing so won't make us smarter.

Weather. Nutrition can't change the weather. What we eat can't make us weather-resistant. What we drink can. Temperature, humidity, wind, and sun — all of these induce or inhibit sweating. The athlete who appreciates the significance of water has a distinct competitive edge (see chapter 8). More contests are lost through dehydration than through any other nutritional shortcoming.

Setting. Whether it's a sandlot or a stadium, where we play has no connection with what we eat. It can have a lot to do with whether we win or lose. There's no nutritional way around the proverbial home-team advantage. (Some practical suggestions for on-the-road eating are given in chapter 15).

Equipment. Rather than spending money on Tiger's Milk, vitamin tablets, protein supplements, and dessicated-liver pills, we would benefit more by spending it on a new piece of equipment. It's more likely to work wonders for our game than all those supplements put together.

*   *   *

As we have just seen, nutrition plays a limited role in athletic performance. Accepting these limitations is the first step in learning the *only* way to eat to win. The ages have produced a bewildering variety of athletic diets — and practically no evidence that any specific training regimen, however widely touted, offers the athlete a true competitive edge. This year's fad is this year's fad. Those who praise the ergogenic powers of bee pollen should know that the ancient Egyptians attributed the same powers to garlic, which they fed to the slaves who built the Great Pyramids at Giza. Garlic has no such powers, of course, but neither does bee pollen, "vitamin B-15," or brewer's yeast. In fact, no special substance or supplement is ever needed by any athlete on a normal, nutritionally balanced diet. As Drs. Clayne R. Jensen and A. Garth Fisher have noted in their book, *The Scientific Basis of Athletic Conditioning,* "The nutritional requirements of the athlete are not much different from those of anyone else. There is no scientific evidence that athletic performance can be improved by modifying a basically sound and nutritious diet." This view should be the basis for a nutritional movement that deserves to be heartily endorsed: the liberation of the American athlete.

If you have ever tried to improve your performance with a pill, a potion, or a powder, if you have ever succumbed to some promise of ergogenic magic, then you've been exploited and manipulated. The moment you put nutrition in perspective and understand its limits, you will join "athletes' lib." You're ready to consider how nutrition *can* make a difference. Sports scientists like Jensen and Fisher, far from closing the door on the nutrition–performance connection, are opening it wider and letting in the light. They couple their assessment of the limits of nutrition with an equally important observation, one that changes the picture entirely.

3

Optimal Nutrition

An athlete can go downhill very rapidly if his diet
is less than optimal.

CLAYNE R. JENSEN
and A. GARTH FISHER
The Scientific Basis of
Athletic Conditioning

The diet we eat today was not planned or developed for any particular purpose. It is a happen-
stance related to our affluence, the productivity of
our farmers and the activities of our food industry.
The risks associated with this diet are demonstra-
bly large.

MARK HESTED,
Director of Nutrition Programs,
United States Department of Agriculture

FEW PEOPLE, ATHLETES INCLUDED, understand what constitutes an adequate diet, let alone an optimal diet. Yet if you deny
yourself the competitive edge of an optimal diet — out of habit,
ignorance, or misinformation — you may be denying yourself the
thrill of an optimal performance. You deserve that thrill. You've
trained hard to win. Now learn how to eat to win by eating an
optimal diet.

The basic requirements for an optimal diet are short and simple:

1. It contains all the nutrients needed to keep you healthy, active, and energetic.

17

2. It provides all the calories needed to maintain your best body weight.

3. It includes foods that you enjoy and that don't disrupt your system.

To this brief list can be added a fourth requirement, one that is not directly connected with nutrition itself:

4. It is composed of foods that are easy to find, easy to prepare, and affordable.

These requirements seem, on first inspection, simple and straightforward enough. But a closer inspection reveals how complex they actually are.

Nutrient Content. Proteins, fats, carbohydrates, vitamins, and minerals — the nutrients needed by the body — can be scientifically identified and measured. *Nutritious,* however, is an extremely flexible concept. Many laboratory animals have been selectively bred to prosper on very specific diets, but no such breeding program has ever been applied to people. As a result, we have very diverse nutritional needs. They vary not only from race to race and ethnic group to ethnic group but even from sibling to sibling. This makes it difficult to define what *nutritious* means for a given person.

Science recognizes many variables that affect an individual's nutritional needs: age, sex, weight, body type, energy expenditure, general health, metabolism, climate, workload, and others. All these factors have been taken into account by many groups, ranging from the Department of Agriculture of the United States to the Food and Agriculture Organization of the United Nations, who issue nutritional guidelines. The Recommended Dietary Allowances (RDAs) given in chapter 10 are those of the Food and Nutrition Board of the National Research Council. They apply only to Americans but are broadly similar to guidelines for countries where the commonly available foods and eating habits differ. The RDAs, like all such measurements, contain generous safety factors that make them adequate for the known nutritional needs of practically every American in practically any circumstance, including the most active athletes.

Nutritional science has shown that virtually no athlete — even one on a less-than-optimal average American diet — needs to worry about meeting the RDAs for essential nutrients. All athletes do need to consider, however, their eating patterns and habits. Why, for example, do Japanese-Americans have a much higher incidence of heart disease than their relatives in Tokyo, Kyoto, and Osaka? The answer seems to be that their diet is much higher in saturated fats than is traditional Japanese cuisine. And why do Finns living in rural northern Karelia have twice as many heart attacks as those who live in Helsinki? Here again, the answer seems to be dietary: the Karelians consume more meat, more butter, and more eggs. Eating patterns, though not the only explanation for these differences, are a significant factor. Study after study has revealed that certain eating patterns are strongly associated with health, longevity, and fitness. These findings are of special importance in defining an optimal diet for athletes, because, with only the most minor exceptions, any dietary change that is known to improve a person's prospects in the long run will also be a day-in, day-out energy and fitness booster.

Caloric Content. Because we are not nutritional clones, our caloric needs are hard to determine. The gap among average males of average weight can be as much as 4000 calories per day. Part of the difference can be attributed to activity patterns: for example, the lumberjack needs more calories than the bank clerk. Yet caloric intake can also vary for athletes in the same sport. If the eating habits of twenty joggers of the same age, sex, and occupation were compared, some would be found to consume twice as many calories per day as others. This holds true even for trained cyclists on identical exercise regimens. Russian volleyball players, who eat 4500–5500 calories per day, would rate the Japanese volleyball players' diet of 3150–3850 calories per day as less than optimal. Yet the Russian team does not overpower the Japanese team with any regularity, an indication that both teams have found the levels of caloric intake at which they perform best.

The calorie question is so complex, and the counting of calories so impractical, that specific recommendations are meaningless. Nevertheless, *overweight, underweight,* and *optimal weight* are simple, practical, and meaningful concepts to every athlete. An optimal diet incorporates the eating patterns that provide the needed calories and nutrients and that allow the desired weight to be maintained.

Enjoyability and Compatibility. Here too the range of human differences is remarkable. Hunger, which is so simple in simple animals, is incredibly subtle and complex in people. The so-called appetite center in the brain is easily and frequently overridden by numerous physical and psychological factors. As a result, our reactions to food are both difficult to predict and hard to direct. A meal that tastes great and "sits" well on one occasion may have the opposite effect on another. And, of course, every individual, ethnic group, and culture has favorite foods that are viewed with outright queasiness by others. The ever-fickle, ever-changing nature of our appetite is not without merit: variety is good for us. All the scientific evidence shows that a high-variety diet is associated with a high level of health, fitness, and vitality. An optimal diet cannot ignore this relationship.

Convenience. Virtually all serious athletes are short of two things: time and money. An optimal diet should take these realities into account. It should consist of affordable foods that can be found in the average supermarket and that can be prepared quickly and easily.

* * *

How, then, can the optimal diet be summarized? Because of the nutritional individuality that characterizes humankind, it is impossible to say what constitutes *the* optimal diet for you. It is possible to say, however, that if you adjust your personal eating habits to conform to certain nutritional patterns, you will be on a personalized optimal diet. It will offer a competitive edge that will make a difference. It will certainly be a diet that will make nutrition as effective as it can be in your performance, your health, and your life.

The Eat-to-Win Plans

For the past seven decades, the Department of Agriculture has released an annual report on our dietary habits. It details our per capita consumption of red meat, milled flour, grain spirits, and so forth. In the late 1970s, the Senate Select Committee on Nutrition released a report entitled *Dietary Goals for the United States*. These are not unrelated publishing events. If the statistics contained in the Department of Agriculture's report had not been so alarming, there would have been no need for the committee to issue its guidelines.

The committee's report calls for a reduction in the consumption of refined sugar, because, according to the Department of Agriculture, sugar consumption has climbed 50 percent since the turn of the century. True, we eat less candy than we used to, but this decrease is more than offset by the amount of sugar that is being added to an increasing number of convenience foods. And, as expert witnesses from the medical community have testified, the more than one hundred pounds of sugar consumed yearly by the average American displaces nutritious foods and increases the chances of obesity and tooth decay.

The report also advises a sharp reduction in salt intake, because statistics show that we consume ten to thirty times the amount we need. As the experts have pointed out, the excess is a time bomb for the 20 percent of us who have a predisposition to hypertension, a predisposition that cannot be detected in advance but that is a danger that can be easily guarded against by reducing salt intake.

Similarly, the report recommends that we reduce our intake of meat. True, the Department of Agriculture has found that we've been eating a little less beef since 1975. But we still eat more meat than people in any other country: an average of over 240 pounds per person per year. This is 30 percent more than the French and Germans, 50 percent more than the British, and a full 100 percent more than the Scandinavians. As the experts have told the senators, the amount of meat we eat is the reason our national diet is so dangerously high in fat, a high-fat diet that has been linked with obesity, heart disease, and some kinds of cancer.

The plain truth is that we are eating too "well" for our own good. Ours is, without question, the richest diet in the world. It may also be the most dangerous of all nutritionally adequate diets because it is so rich, so much more than merely adequate.

There was a time in the not-so-distant past when it was almost impossible to imagine a diet that was too rich. Many of our attitudes toward what we eat and how we eat date from that time. Indeed, most of our ancestors came to this country not in search of religious toleration but in search of an adequate diet. They were refugees from the potato famines of Ireland, the crop failures of

Eastern Europe, the droughts of North Africa. They came to the United States not because they had heard that the streets were paved with gold but because they had heard that there was a chicken for every pot.

For the most part, this is a promise that the United States has kept. There are no potato famines here. Starvation is as rare here as it is commonplace in several Third World nations. But the memory of the days of deprivation lingers on. We still think of poultry and beef as special foods, when in fact they are such an ordinary part of our diet that they have become *the* staple, having replaced bread as the staff of life. So we consume both in quantity, heedless of the threat this pattern poses to our health.

No one, least of all the Senate committee, is suffering an attack of nostalgia for the good old days, which had their own set of nutritional problems. The decision in the 1930s to fortify milk with vitamins A and D effectively eliminated the persistent problem of rickets. The development of chemical preservatives has extended the shelf life of foods that were once unavailable on a regular basis and at affordable prices. Enriching bread and cereals with the vitamins removed during modern processing does not replace the taste or the fiber. But it is a solution that has virtually eliminated vitamin-deficiency diseases in this country. Although modern techniques of plant genetics, cultivation, harvesting, and shipping may result in such dubious advances as the tasteless tomato, they also guarantee a year-round supply of fresh produce at prices the average consumer can afford.

Any nutritionist will say that there was also a lot of nutritional good in the good old days. Those were the days before corn-fed beef, before breakfast cereals with the sugar content of candy, before heat-and-serve entrées and convenience foods larded with fat and loaded with salt. The American diet was not as rich in those days, but in many ways, it was better. No one is advocating a return to the nutritional deficiencies of bygone times, but everyone is advocating a return to the nutritional patterns of those times.

Whether or not we're aware of it or admit it, the illustration at right describes our eating habits fairly accurately. You might think that you eat more sensibly than the figure illustrates if you avoid junk food, take supplements, or eat only fertilized eggs, raw milk, honey, and organic vegetables. But such a regimen

How We Eat

Fat 42%	Saturated fats 16%
	Unsaturated fats 26%
Protein 12%	12%
Carbohydrates 46%	Complex carbohydrates 22%
	Sugar 24%

doesn't necessarily mean eating better, even when it includes foods that are hard to find, time-consuming to prepare, or expensive.

Surveys have shown that athletes, except those who have begun to discover the ergogenic advantages of a high-carbohydrate diet, have no better nutritional knowledge or eating patterns than other people. Some athletes, armed with that most dangerous thing — a little knowledge — even put themselves at a greater nutritional disadvantage. They eat an excessive amount of meat protein and get the accompanying excessive amount of fat. (They may even be forcing their bodies to do what they least want: burn protein for fuel.) They consume sugar during competition, hoping for a quick energy boost but getting only superfluous calories and, in fairly short order, an energy letdown. The result is a diet that is skewed even further in the direction of protein, fat, and sugar. Such a diet is not the average American diet. It's one that is distinctly worse.

What we should be aiming for, according to the Senate committee, is the diet shown in the illustration below. Fat and sugar are significantly reduced; complex carbohydrates are significantly increased; and protein remains the same. In practical terms, this requires cutting our consumption of meat and high-fat dairy products so as to reduce our intake of saturated fats; decreasing our intake of unsaturated fats and vegetable oils; drastically reducing our sugar

How We Should Eat

Fat 30%	Saturated fats 10%
	Unsaturated fats 20%
Protein 12%	12%
Carbohydrates 58%	Complex carbohydrates 43%
	Sugar 15%

consumption; and doubling our intake of grain products, vegetables, and fruits — a shift that automatically increases the amount of fiber in our diet and provides protein. The committee also suggests lowering our sodium intake by not using table salt and/or by limiting our consumption of highly salted foods, and decreasing our cholesterol intake by restricting the number of eggs we eat.

The irony is that How We Should Eat almost perfectly describes how we ate at the turn of the century. There are differences in preparation and storage — for example, today, few of us bake our own bread, skim our own milk, or keep a root cellar or a larder — but the composition is very nearly the same. Both diets are low in fats and sugar and high in fruits, grains, and vegetables.

Not surprisingly, each of the committee's recommendations has met with vigorous opposition. Cattlemen, for example, are appalled at the suggestion that we decrease our consumption of saturated animal fats. Sugar companies, which have no opinion on saturated fats, are shocked at the suggestion that we reduce our intake of refined sugar by 40 percent. And the egg industry, though expressing no sympathy for cattlemen or sugar refiners, is dismayed by the committee's recommendation that adult males avoid eggs as a way of reducing their cholesterol intake.

No one, however, has come forward to champion the cause of salt, the oldest of condiments and the earliest known food additive, even though it gets the worst drubbing at the committee's hands. Noting that salt predisposes heavy users to hypertension and that its overuse has been connected with migraine headaches, heart disease, and stomach cancer, the committee declares that salt should be virtually eliminated as a table seasoning.

Salt is but one member of what the dean of American nutritionists, Jean Mayer of Tufts University, calls nutrition's deadly trinity. The other two are cholesterol and sugar. Unhappily, even the harsh illumination of a Senate hearing room could shed little new light on the question of cholesterol, an issue that has engaged the interest, and sometimes quickened the tempers, of some of the best minds in the scientific community. The so-called diet–heart controversy is so complex that most of chapter 7 is devoted to it.

About the last member of Mayer's trinity — sugar — there is controversy but there shouldn't be. Some food faddists lay every dietary ill at sugar's door. The people who profit from the sale of sugar, on the other hand, laud its "instant-energy" potential. Obesity and tooth decay are as real as instant energy is illusory, but mentioning their relationship to high sugar consumption obscures the real issue: sugar is superfluous. It is not an essential nutrient; rather, it is an additive. It contributes nothing to the diet but calories. If you work out strenuously and consume, say, 4500 calories per day to maintain your body weight, you can afford the empty calories of refined sugar, but even you don't need them. The body is designed to manufacture — and operates best when it gets — all the sugar it needs from the complex carbohydrates in grains, vegetables, and fruits. Recognizing this, the committee calls for a sharp reduction in sugar consumption. But because it also recognizes that we have a well-nurtured "sweet tooth," which goes all the way back to baby formula, it pegs the goal at a reduction of 40 percent. This, it feels, is the high side of tolerable. Seventy percent, which is better from a medical standpoint, is deemed too stringent.

The committee's report, which links the way we eat with six of the ten major killers — heart disease, cancer, stroke, diabetes, arteriosclerosis, and cirrhosis of the liver — may be under attack by the special-interest groups who stand to lose if its goals are attained. But the medical community is in broad agreement that the goals are both sensible and necessary. As reported in the *Journal of the American Medical Association*, a survey of two hundred scientists set the following dietary priorities: to eat less in general; to eat less fat in particular, and more specifically less animal fat; to lower the intake of cholesterol, sugar, and salt; to increase the consumption of fiber-rich complex carbohydrates.

The World Health Organization suggests the following dietary parameters for athletes: 22–33 percent fat, 13–15 percent protein, and 50–55 percent carbohydrates. Because both this diet and the How We Should Eat diet promote longevity, well-being, and vitality, either can be highly recommended as a basic athletic diet. They are vast improvements over the How We Eat diet and will carry us far toward the goal of optimal nutrition. Some athletes may want and need something more, however. One of the two Eat-to-Win plans outlined below — one for basic training, the other for intensive training — will suit their needs.

The Eat-to-Win Basic Training plan calls for a further reduction

Eat to Win

Basic-Training Diet

Fat 20%	Saturated fats 7%
	Unsaturated fats 13%
Protein 12%	12%
Carbohydrates 68%	Complex carbohydrates 58%
	Sugar 10%

Intensive-Training Diet

Fat 15%	Saturated fats 5%
	Unsaturated fats 10%
Protein 12%	12%
Carbohydrates 73%	Complex carbohydrates 68%
	Sugar 5%

in fat and sugar and an increase in complex carbohydrates, the dietary form of the most important high-performance fuel. The plan requires the following:

1. Favoring foods that are fresh or lightly processed (in order to avoid the hidden fat, sugar, and salt so often found in canned, convenience, and fast foods).
2. Increasing the use of grains (bread, cereal, pasta, rice), potatoes, and beans (sources of complex carbohydrates and protein).
3. Eating meat less often or in smaller servings.
4. Using low-fat milk products.

5. Favoring foods that have been steamed, poached, baked, boiled, or broiled rather than fried.

6. Flavoring foods with low-fat, low-salt seasonings, sauces, dips, and dressings.

7. Eating low-fat, low-salt snacks.

8. Eating low-sugar, low-fat desserts.

If some or most of these requirements mean that you have to give up many of your favorite foods, then How We Eat is how you eat. There is no question that to eat to win, you must make some adjustments in your eating patterns. If you follow some of the above guidelines all of the time, or most of them some of the time, then you will easily attain the Senate committee's goals for How We Should Eat. Yet even the Basic Training plan leaves room for indulgences. On a nutrients-per-calorie basis, highly processed foods, fried foods, sugary foods and drinks, and snack foods have the least going for them. (Some painless substitutes are suggested in chapters 13 and 14.) If you eat one of these a day, it won't jeopardize your training goals, but eating two may, and eating three will. Even then, what will count most is the overall thrust of your training. Patterns and habits matter far more than any specific break in training. Breaking training is a problem only when it becomes the pattern.

If you've been breaking training too often, if you're looking for a high-energy weight-loss program, or if you're the type who always goes all out, take a look at the Intensive Training plan. In fairness, you should be told that you'll find it challenging. It calls for an even sharper reduction in fat and sugar and a corresponding increase in complex carbohydrates. This means almost totally eliminating added fat and sugar, cutting meat intake by three-fourths, and strictly adhering to the basic-training guidelines listed above. In return, you will get a maximum amount of energy and nutrients for every calorie you consume. For these reasons, the Intensive Training plan is also an ideal weight-loss regimen — and an ideal weight-maintenance plan for athletes who want minimum body weight or body fat. For many other athletes, it can be an effective shock treatment for taste buds numbed by excess fat, sugar, and salt. In fact, three days on the Intensive Training plan practically guarantees that How We Eat will never again be how you eat.

The How We Should Eat diet and the Eat-to-Win Basic Training and Intensive Training plans differ only in degree; their thrust is the same. One of these regimens is right for you. But which one and at which times, only you can determine. The upcoming nutritional information will help you decide, starting with an easy way to take your own nutritional measure.

4

Assessing Your Nutritional Needs

> Fortunate, indeed, is the man who takes exactly
> the right measure of himself, and holds a just bal-
> ance between what he can acquire and what he
> can use, be it great or be it small!
>
> PETER MERE LATHAM
> (1789–1875)

NUTRITION IS JUST ONE of many factors that affect our performance, well-being, and longevity. But it is an important one, one
that is directly and indirectly related to the other factors. Although
it is impossible to measure the effects of nutrition precisely, it is
possible to estimate the extent to which a less-than-optimal diet is
preventing us from fulfilling our potential — in life in general, and
in sports in particular.

The questions below and the comments that follow will help you
make such an estimate. They will allow you to assess your nutritional needs against the backdrop of your lifestyle, heredity, and
current level of fitness and health. They will help you assess your
current eating patterns. They will also show you how interrelated
nutrition is with health, fitness, and performance — in ways that
may surprise you. By the time you reach the end of this chapter,
you will know whether, and how, nutrition could be doing more
for you.

* * *

1. Rate Your Sport
How physically demanding is your sport?

Extremely demanding (extended periods of maximum output): all long-distance sports, including running, swimming, cycling, cross-country skiing, speed skating, rowing; also decathlon, pentathlon. (5 points)

Very demanding (almost constant motion with bursts of maximum effort): ballet, basketball, football, gymnastics, handball, soccer, squash, hockey, field hockey, lacrosse, racquetball, rowing, rugby, swimming, mountaineering, most track events, white-water canoeing, wrestling. (4 points)

Moderately demanding (constant but moderate effort, or intermittently intensive effort): calisthenics, canoeing, downhill skiing, hiking, fencing, figure skating, jogging, martial arts, recreational bicycling, surfing, tennis, volleyball, weightlifting, most field events. (3 points)

Slightly demanding (intermittent activity with opportunities for rest): badminton, baseball, bowling, golf (if you walk), Ping-Pong, polo, sailing, roller skating. (2 points)

Not demanding (minimum effort, with emphasis on skill): archery, billiards, cricket, croquet, fishing, golf (if you ride), horseback riding, skeet shooting. (1 point)

SCORE: _____

2. Rate Your Fitness

A. How often do you exercise, work out, practice, or play?
Once a week or only on weekends. (5 points)
Two or three times a week. (3 points)
Every day or almost every day. (1 point)

A: _____

B. How hard do you exercise, work out, practice, or play?
Extremely hard; I push myself to the limit. (5 points)
Very hard, but I pace myself. (4 points)
Steadily, with occasional bursts of hard playing. (3 points)

Steadily. (2 points)

Not very hard; I don't push myself. (1 point)

B: ———

SCORE (A × B): ———

3. Rate Your Body Type
Which description best fits you?

I can't remember when I didn't have a weight problem. I was big and husky even in first grade. (5 points)

I'm solid but a bit soft in the gut. (4 points)

I'm a junior hulk, a bulldog, a fire hydrant. I'm built like a tank, solid as a tree trunk — a natural-born linebacker. (3 points)

I'm somewhere between beanpole and bulldog. (2 points)

I'm a beanpole, a 98-pound weakling. Try as I might, I've never been able to bulk up. I'm scrawny, but wiry. (1 point)

SCORE: ———

4. Rate Your Age
How old are you?

40 or older. (6 points)

30–39. (3 points)

20–29. (2 points)

19 or younger. (1 point)

SCORE: ———

5. Rate Your Genes
A. How many people in your family have lived to a ripe old age?

Hardly any. (5 points)

A few. (4 points)

More than a few. (3 points)

Many. (2 points)

Just about all. (1 point)

A: ———

B. How many members of your family (parents, grandparents, siblings, aunts, and uncles) have or have had a heart attack, hardening of the arteries, lung disease, hypertension, high blood pressure, diabetes, or a stroke?

>More than two. (5 points)
>One or two. (3 points)
>None. (1 point)

B: _____

SCORE (A + B): _____

6. Rate Your Health

A. Do you have, or have you had, any of the following: rheumatic heart disease, hypertension, high blood pressure, arthritis or other rheumatic diseases, diabetes, ulcer, inflammatory bowel disease, coronary heart disease, allergies, or asthma?

>Yes.
>No.

(NO SCORE — SEE COMMENTS)

B. Do you regularly take one or more prescription drugs?

>Yes.
>No.

(NO SCORE — SEE COMMENTS)

C. How accurately does each of the following describe you? (1 point: perfectly; 2 points: fairly accurately; 3 points: more or less; 4 points: not especially; 5 points: not at all)

>I'm as healthy as a horse. I never seem to get sick.

_____

>I have a cast-iron stomach. I can eat anything.

_____

SCORE: _____

7. Rate Your Stress Level

A. Which statement best describes you?

>I suspect I'm always overstressed and rarely relaxed. (10 points)

>Long-range personal problems create a lot of stress for me, and I have trouble putting these problems aside. (7 points)

I have a high-pressure lifestyle but I handle the pressures fairly well. (5 points)

My life has its stresses and strains. They get me down sometimes but not for long. (3 points)

I have a low-key lifestyle, and I'm naturally easygoing. (1 point)

A: _____

B. How many "yes" answers do you have to the following? (1 point for each)

Behind in your work? Failing, flunked, skipped a grade, passed over or promoted? Is your performance "good enough"? Are you an outsider or a loner? Recently engaged, married, a parent, separated, divorced, widowed? Living alone? Worried about money, heavily in debt, bankrupt, in litigation? Any health worries? Sick a lot? Any stress-related diseases? Impotent, frigid, asexual, oversexed, menopausal? In therapy? In mourning? In a hurry? Always late? Often impatient?

B: _____

SCORE (A + B): _____

8. Rate Your "Bad" Habits

A. On the average, how many of each of the following do you drink a day? (1 point for each)

Beers. _____

Glasses of wine. _____

Mixed drinks. _____

B. On the average, how many cigarettes do you smoke a day?

More than ten. (5 points) _____

Ten or fewer. (2 points) _____

None. (1 point) _____

C. Add A and B unless A is 0 or B is 1. _____

D. On the average, how many times a day do you smoke marijuana? (2 points for each time) _____

SCORE: (A + B + C + D): _____

9. Rate Your Weight

How many of the following statements apply to you? (1 point for each)

I'm not always satisfied with my weight.

When I diet, I seem to have no energy.

My weight is constantly fluctuating, sometimes by as much as ten or fifteen pounds a year.

I have tried one or more of the following diets: Stillman, Atkins, Scarsdale, Air Force, Drinking Man's, "Mayo," Calories Don't Count, 10-Day Wonder.

I would do better at my sport if I weighed less.

I have trouble making weight for my sport.

I've tried one or more of the following: over-the-counter or prescription diet pills, diuretics, liquid protein, Ayds, and so forth.

SCORE: _____

10. Rate Your Eating Habits

A. On the average, how many servings of each of the following do you have a day? (1 point for each serving)

Whole milk. _____

Cheese, cream, sour cream. _____

Ice cream. _____

Butter or margarine. _____

Bacon, ham, sausage. _____

Bologna, luncheon meat. _____

Salad dressing. _____

Fried foods (including chicken, chops,
French fries, deep-fried vegetables). _____

Nuts. _____

B. On the average, how many servings of each of the following do you have a day?

Sugar (in coffee or tea, for example) _____

Breakfast cereal. _____

Jelly, jam, and so forth (on toast or
muffins, for example) _____

Soft drinks. _____

Cookies, brownies, candy bars (including
"health bars"). _____

Pie, cake, and other desserts of any sort. _____

Ketchup. _____

    C. On the average, how many servings of each of the following
do you have a day?

Canned soups, canned sauces. _____

Canned vegetables. _____

Boil-in-bag and heat-and-serve
convenience foods. _____

Cured meats (ham, bacon, and so forth). _____

Pretzels, chips, crackers. _____

Canned tomato juice, V-8 Juice. _____

Soy sauce, Worcestershire sauce, hot
sauce. _____

Table salt (that is, how many times do
you use the salt shaker?) _____

    D. Do you take vitamin and mineral supplements?

Yes. (5 points)

No. (0 points)

_____

SCORE (A + B + C + D): _____

TOTAL SCORE: _____

Comments

1. *Rate Your Sport.* Peak performance in any sport requires
skill, strength, and stamina, but saying this is as basic as saying
that a cake recipe calls for sugar, flour, and eggs. For sports as well
as for cakes, it's the way the ingredients are combined that's important. For example, some sports place a far greater demand on
the heart and lungs than on the muscles. The reverse is true for
some others. And a few, the so-called skill-intensive sports, tax the
eye and hand enormously but tire the body scarcely at all. Talent
and skill are ultimately far more important than fitness in these
sports. (This is why there's plenty of paunch in professional baseball and golf.)

If you scored 3, 4, or 5 points on this question, your sport is energy-intensive. It requires a great output of energy, probably for long periods. Optimal nutrition will maximize your energy reserves for training and for performance. If your score is 1 or 2 points, your sport is one of those that require far more skill than strength or stamina. Although optimal nutrition is not essential for peak performance, it will promote longevity and good health.

2. *Rate Your Fitness.* Being an athlete doesn't necessarily mean being fit.

If your score was 9 points or less, you're either very fit, because you exercise often and take exercise seriously, or very out of shape, because you are casual about exercising. In the first case, good nutrition can complement your superior conditioning program by increasing your energy reserves. In the second case, it will promote the maximal well-being that is possible without regular, strenuous exercise, but you will do well to consider exercising regularly.

A score of 15 points or more, on the other hand, suggests that you may be endangering yourself every time you exercise. Because you are playing too hard too infrequently, you may be making yourself a candidate for a heart attack. You will profit by exercising *regularly.* And you will certainly benefit from optimal nutrition, which is low in fats and cholesterol.

Remember, if you are over thirty-five, have been inactive for more than five years, or have a family history of heart disease, you should see your doctor before you begin any exercise program. A number of tests may be in order to determine how strenuously you can safely exercise at the outset.

3. *Rate Your Body Type.* If you scored 1 or 2 points, you're an ectomorph. Although you might lament your lack of bulk, longevity experts do not. Your physique is the best type for endurance sports — and for endurance in life. Optimal nutrition will contribute to peak performance by building the energy reserves you require to go the distance. If, on the other hand, you scored 5 points or even 4, you're an endomorph — and prone to lifelong weight problems. Optimal nutrition will help you too, for it can aid in reaching and/or maintaining your desired weight. This is of critical importance, both on and off the playing field. If your score is 3 points, you're a mesomorph, and your body is well suited for build-

ing strength and muscle. Although optimal nutrition is not essential for doing this, it will contribute to your overall well-being. In addition, today's mesomorphs have a way of becoming tomorrow's endomorphs — when they stop exercising vigorously and settle into sedentary lifestyles. Establishing good eating habits now will enable you to avoid weight problems later.

4. *Rate Your Age.* There is no hard evidence that good eating and exercise patterns prolong life. But there are good reasons to believe that they contribute to the quality of life.

In youth, the reserves of the organs that sustain life, such as the heart and lungs, are more than ten times what they need to be. This is why young people are so resilient and bounce back so readily from nutritional and physical abuses. The reserves, which are essential for coping with the stresses and strains of life, start to decline around the age of thirty. Once the decline begins, it continues, steadily and inevitably. Anyone who survives diseases and accidents will eventually reach an age when stress can be fatal.

In 1900, the average American life span was forty-seven years. Today, it's seventy-three, but even this figure is lower than for many other Western countries. Researchers believe that the potential average upper limit is between eighty-five and ninety-five. But do we really want to live longer if we can't delay the onset of the physical and mental deterioration associated with old age? Well, research is providing evidence that we can: by making changes in our lifestyles, especially in the way we eat and exercise. By staying active and eating wisely, the decline in our physical reserves can be slowed by as much as 50 percent — more than enough to keep us ripe in old age.

Even if you scored 6 points — that is, if you're forty or older — it isn't too late to improve your eating habits and increase your chance for a longer, more satisfying life. Of course, the sooner you start, the more time you will have to enjoy the many benefits of optimal nutrition.

5. *Rate Your Genes.* Although regular exercise, a positive outlook, a satisfying lifestyle, and optimal nutrition all contribute to the quality of life, a great deal of our destiny has been written in our genes. The current thinking is that our genes don't help us live longer but that they do limit our life spans by predisposing us to certain diseases. You are more likely to develop certain health

problems, including those mentioned in B, if they run in your family.

If you have a superior genetic makeup — that is, if you scored 3 or less — you may be able to take a lot of abuse, nutritional and otherwise, yet outlast everyone else. But why take the risk? If you scored higher, don't be dismayed. You could still have the last laugh if you eat wisely and exercise regularly — the two steps that experts say can keep a predisposition from becoming a condition.

6. *Rate Your Health.* Health and fitness are not the same. It is possible for someone to be in superb physical condition and to be sick at the same time: a ranking marathon runner with a bad head cold, for example. And it is possible (less likely, admittedly, but possible) to be in good shape from a doctor's point of view yet in wretched shape from a trainer's point of view.

As Catfish Hunter, a diabetic, can tell us, health problems don't necessarily limit a person's ability to excel in athletics. Yet they do pose problems that other athletes don't face. Knowing how to deal with them is of prime importance. And many health problems can be treated or controlled, at least in part, by diet, but only under a doctor's supervision.

If you answered yes to A or B, consult your doctor before making *any* change in your routine. You're probably already on a special diet, so you're aware that nutrition is important to you. It may be that nutrition could be doing even more for you. If you are interested in one of the regimens suggested in later chapters, your doctor will probably find that it meets or exceeds his or her dietary recommendations.

7. *Rate Your Stress Level.* Stress is anything — good or bad, welcome or unwelcome, physical or mental — that places a demand on the body. It is often evident in our behavior, attitude, and emotions: pregame jitters, the single-mindedness that accompanies intense competition, the joy of victory or the agony of defeat. Whatever the source, stress always has physiological effects: it increases heart rate, blood pressure, hormone levels, respiration, muscle tension.

Stress is unavoidable, and physical stress — exercise — is essential to well-being. Nevertheless, although the body is well equipped to handle the everyday stresses of life, stress can be dangerous —

even deadly — especially if we are unaware of it or are unable to deal with it.

Some people thrive on nonstop stress. They don't get ulcers; they cause them. And some people always seem to be able to put their cares aside long enough to relax. However, some high-pressure people with high-pressure lifestyles are totally unaware of the chronic stress of their lives and find no outlet for reducing the tension. They have a much greater chance of developing one or more stress-related ailments, such as headache, backache, arthritis, asthma, allergy, diabetes, ulcer, stroke, heart disease, and possibly even cancer. Thus, how well we identify stress and how well we deal with it are more important than the amount of stress we are under.

To the extent that you scored above 10 points, you are a high-stress individual and you can benefit from some of the proven ways to reduce stress: exercising for cardiovascular fitness, making changes in your lifestyle, meditation and biofeedback, counselling or therapy, certain prescription drugs. Any or all of these can be effective. For example, even twenty minutes of sustained exercise — brisk walking, cycling, jogging, swimming — three times a week can lower your blood pressure and increase your cardiovascular efficiency.

Can optimal nutrition also play a part in helping you deal with stress? There is no clearcut answer. Good nutrition increases our resistance to disease in general. But research is still trying to determine the exact connections between diet, stress, and disease. Certainly, one aspect of stressful living is poor eating patterns. So working on improving the way you eat is an important part of any stress-management program.

8. *Rate Your "Bad" Habits.* There is some evidence that a couple of drinks a day may be good for us, because such moderate drinking is associated with a lower risk of heart disease. But a couple of additional drinks will probably affect our training and performance, and a couple beyond that definitely will. So, if you scored 3 points or more on A, reducing the amount you drink will remove empty calories from your diet and improve your endurance and heat tolerance.

What are tobacco and marijuana doing in a nutrition questionnaire? They're not here because cigarettes can be a food substitute, or because marijuana can cause the munchies, or even because one out of three athletes smokes. They're here because nothing negates the endurance-building benefits of optimal nutrition more than what we put in our lungs. Lung cancer and heart disease are the top two long-term risks from smoking. But of immediate concern to athletes interested in endurance is smoking's effect on their wind, its restriction of the amount of oxygen that gets into the bloodstream and to the muscles. Studies of habitual marijuana smokers show similar results: higher heart rates, and more pulmonorespiratory disorders, such as emphysema, bronchitis, and asthma.

Finally, tobacco and alcohol are synergistic. Smokers who drink, for example, have a higher risk of developing cancer of the esophagus, larynx, throat, and mouth.

If your total score for this section is 6 points or more, your health may be perfectly normal. But what's normal in our society leaves considerable room for improvement. And if you're an athlete interested in endurance, keep in mind that nothing you eat can offset the negative effects of what you drink and smoke.

9. *Rate Your Weight.* In general, the overweight that plagues one of every three adult Americans is not a problem faced by active athletes. But if your weight worries you, put your concern in perspective. Even an extra twenty to thirty pounds poses no known health problems. True, surplus fat is nourished by extra blood vessels and so increases the heart's workload. But studies of overweight people show they unconsciously compensate by reducing their activity levels. Obesity — usually defined as 35 percent above the average — is a health problem, however. In adults, obesity can contribute to high blood pressure, high serum cholesterol, and adult-onset diabetes, all of which are factors in heart disease. Obesity has also been linked to gout, gallstones, and some kinds of cancer, but whether obesity is a direct cause or an aggravating factor is not yet known. If obese people have no signs of the above problems, however, there is no evidence that they will have shorter lives than people of average weight.

Overweight and obese athletes, of course, have an immediate disadvantage: their excess weight slows them down. So if you scored 2 points or even 1, the first thing you need to ask is the most obvious: Are you actually overweight? The mirror will generally give an honest answer. Or look at the following table. It takes your sex, height, and frame size into account, but not your age. Although most people gain weight as they age, this is neither necessary nor ideal. In fact, most health experts feel that your ideal weight in early adulthood is your best weight for life.

Tables such as this one are of limited usefulness for many athletes. Distance runners, dancers, and gymnasts, for example, value a lean, lithe physique, one that may make them technically underweight. Wrestlers, boxers, and weightlifters, on the other hand, have the challenge of making weight. They want the competitive advantage of maximum strength at a minimum weight. And linebackers, shot-putters, and bodybuilders want maximum strength and/or size, and they may be technically overweight. Thus, the real issue in many sports is not body weight but body fat.

Approximate Desirable Weights

Women

Height	Weight		
	Small Frame[1]	Medium Frame[1]	Large Frame[1]
5' 0"	100	109	118
5' 1"	104	112	121
5' 2"	107	115	125
5' 3"	110	118	128
5' 4"	113	122	132
5' 5"	116	125	135
5' 6"	120	129	139
5' 7"	123	132	142
5' 8"	126	136	146
5' 9"	130	140	151
5'10"	133	144	156
5'11"	137	148	161
6' 0"	141	152	166

Men

Height	Weight		
	Small Frame[1]	Medium Frame[1]	Large Frame[1]
5' 3"	118	129	141
5' 4"	122	133	145
5' 5"	126	137	149
5' 6"	130	142	155
5' 7"	134	147	161
5' 8"	139	151	166
5' 9"	143	155	170
5'10"	147	159	174
5'11"	150	163	178
6' 0"	154	167	183
6' 1"	158	171	188
6' 2"	162	175	192
6' 3"	165	178	195

Source: U.S. Department of Agriculture.

1. For most women, a wrist circumference of 5½ inches indicates a small frame; 6 inches a medium frame; and 6½ inches a large frame. For most men, a wrist circumference of 6½ inches indicates a small frame; 7 inches a medium frame; and 7½ inches a large frame.

Hydrostatic (underwater) weighing, which is a commonly used technique in sports laboratories, measures body fat precisely. The technique is straightforward but relatively time-consuming and expensive.

The pinch test is an easier yet fairly exact way to determine body fat. You can have this test made by an expert with calipers, but you can probably learn what you need to know by doing it yourself. Use your thumb and forefinger as pinchers. Grasp a fold of skin at several of the following places: the back of your upper arm, the side of your waist, below the navel on your stomach, the front of your thigh, and one of your buttocks. If the average thickness is less than a half-inch, you're definitely lean. If it's more than an inch, you're definitely fat.

The higher your score on this question, the more dissatisfied you are with your body weight or body fat. Optimal nutrition can help you reach and maintain your desired weight — and to do so without jeopardizing your energy level.

10. *Rate Your Eating Habits.* If you scored 5 points or more on A, you're getting too many calories from fat. A high-fat diet is one of the most important causes of heart disease, which is epidemic in this country. A low-fat diet not only protects you from heart disease, it's a safe and effective way for athletes to lose pounds without sacrificing energy.

If you scored 5 points or more on B, you're getting too many calories from refined sugar, the one substance in our diet that has no nutritional value whatsoever. It is not a source of instant energy, as many athletes think, but only of empty calories. Sugar's intense, concentrated sweetness makes it difficult to appreciate nature's nutritious sweets: fresh fruits. And sugar is the primary cause of tooth decay.

A score of 3 points or more on C means that your salt intake is too high. The body needs the sodium that is in salt, but in nowhere near the amounts supplied by a typical American diet. The excess is dangerous for anyone with a genetic predisposition to high blood pressure, a condition that afflicts 20 percent of Americans.

If you scored 5 points on D, you're among the one of every three Americans who take supplements, even though there is absolutely no evidence that they do a bit of good. What vitamin and minerals can do, however, is give people a false sense of nutritional security.

In fact, they do nothing to offset or correct the real nutritional problems posed by the American way of eating.

*   *   *

Now it's time to do some simple arithmetic. Total your scores in the ten categories. If the total is 20 points or less, you're probably a nonsmoking, nondrinking octogenarian pool player who walks five miles to the pool hall every day, and walks home to a meal of steamed vegetables, whole grains, and dried fruits. Everyone else will fall within the following ranges.

21–40 points. You have so much going for you already that either you have no particular need for optimal nutrition, or you're eating right already.

41–60 points. You're in the grey zone. Should you invest the modest amount of time and effort it will take you to improve your nutritional habits? You probably have enough people telling you what you should be doing. So make up your own mind.

61 points and over. To the extent that your score exceeds 60, you could use some definite advice: you have many good reasons to eat to win, unless you enjoy being a loser. So wise up and change the way you eat.

It's axiomatic that if you want to reach the top of your sport, or the peak of personal fitness and performance, you need the best of all possible diets. So whatever your score, you can benefit from optimal nutrition.

PART TWO

The Components of Nutrition

5

Protein and the Myth of Meat

The relationship between protein intake and physical performance is usually dismissed in a few sentences — as being nonexistent.

THEODORE VAN ITALLIE
Chief, Division of Metabolism
and Nutrition
St. Luke's–Roosevelt Hospital Center
Columbia University

Athletes who think they can improve their performance with protein are victims of one of the oldest myths in sports.

HERMAN J. JOHNSON
Letterman Army Institute of Research
San Francisco, California

THE VENERATION OF PROTEIN, particularly in the form of meat, and more particularly in the form of red meat, is as old as athletics. But the regular consumption of enormous quantities of meat protein is a much more recent — and almost entirely American — phenomenon. The average American eats far more than his or her weight in meat every year. This amount is far in excess of what is needed for optimal health and performance, and *the excess may be harmful to both*. To correct the imbalance and to put meat in its proper perspective, it is necessary to understand how the myth originated.

47

As previously noted, prehistoric hunters sought to acquire the physical prowess of faster, stronger animals by eating them. Our ancestors clearly believed in "muscle to muscle," and that conviction survives today. Yet this alone does not account for the primacy of meat protein in our diet. Scarcity is another factor.

For the most part, our prehistoric ancestors subsisted on a diet of nuts, tubers, fruits, and grains. Gathering and scavenging were much more dependable as sources of food than hunting. When our ancestors did succeed in bringing home the bacon, it was a special occasion, not just because such an event was infrequent but also because it marked another victory over the faster, stronger animals they envied and feared. Thus, meat was the symbol of human superiority. In celebration, and in the knowledge that meat would spoil and that it might not reappear soon on the menu, our ancestors gorged themselves. Their diet was haphazard and lopsided, far from the balanced ideal we strive for today, but it did help them survive. And we now understand why. It aided survival not because meat is high in protein, which the body cannot store, but because it is high in fat, which the body can store. It was stored fat from the feast that protected our ancestors from famine and gave the women the reserves they needed to survive the rigors of pregnancy, childbirth, and nursing.

The development of agriculture and the domestication of animals, events that mark the beginning of civilization, stabilized the food supply — and formalized the myth of meat. It was and still is inefficient to kill the chicken that lays the eggs or the cow that makes the milk (and more cows). The survival needs of civilization dictated an essentially ovo-lacto vegetarian diet (that is, a vegetarian diet that includes eggs and milk). A fatted calf might be slain to celebrate the prodigal son's return. Otherwise, a calf was far too valuable as a potential source of milk to be slaughtered until its productive life was over, when its hide as well as its less tender but no less nutritious meat could be used.

Like any scarce commodity, meat acquired status. It became associated with royalty, wealth, privilege, and ceremony. Short of a human sacrifice, an animal was the ultimate offering to the gods, for its loss represented a real sacrifice to all but the wealthiest. As part of a herd, it was a tangible buffer against the cycle of feast and famine. When the herd thrived, the tribe thrived. If we add this significance to the prehistoric meanings of meat — a source of animal prowess and a symbol of human superiority — we have the myth of meat.

It was not until the settlement of North America, however, that the myth found expression in the regular consumption of meat. The wilderness teemed with game. Land, when it wasn't free, was cheap. New farms had more than enough room for domestic animals and more than enough fodder to feed them. In this land of plenty, a near-vegetarian diet was a matter of choice rather than necessity. Everyone could eat like a king. When Dr. Alexander Hamilton, one of the more refined inhabitants of Baltimore (and no relation to the Founding Father), toured the colonies in 1744, he was shocked by the forwardness of his "inferiors." But he had to share their fare: "fry'd chickens and bacon" in Maryland, "veal, beef stakes, and raspberries" in New York. The fatted calf had become standard fare — and another potent force had been added to the myth of meat: habit.

Tradition and habit have stamped meat with the seal of approval. For a while, so did science. The conviction that red meat has particular ergogenic properties can be traced, in written history at least, as far back as 450 B.C. to Dromeus of Stymphalus. He was convinced that the Olympic competitors of his day could improve their performance by eating the power-supplying muscles of powerful animals. This muscle-to-muscle concept remained the commonly accepted theory for more than two thousand years. Somehow — by a process still to be discovered — muscle was believed to be destroyed during exercise. It seemed to follow logically that muscle should be replaced by eating muscle. But not until nutrition emerged as a science in the 1800s was this long-accepted idea finally tested.

Antoine Lavoisier, a French chemist of the revolutionary period, was the first to perceive food as a fuel. By the early 1800s, Lavoisier's followers had determined the protein, fat, carbohydrate, and mineral content of most foodstuffs and of body tissue as well. Muscle, it turned out, was primarily protein. Because the body supposedly burned protein for fuel during exercise, protein was naturally thought to be needed to replace it. This idea — really just a sophisticated version of the muscle-to-muscle concept — was advanced by Justus von Leibeg, the German nobleman who is now remembered for his contributions to modern chemistry. In his time, however, he was famous for his special athletic diet, which combined red meat (to replace the protein burned during exercise), bread, mild beer, and strong purges.

In the 1860s, the rowing crews at Oxford University adopted the von Leibeg diet, sensibly omitting the purges and adding tea. Throughout the decade, Oxford racked up an unbroken string of victories over archrival Cambridge. Credit for those victories was duly accorded to the most exotic variable: the von Leibeg diet. No one thought to credit the more probable but prosaic variables: Oxford's superior talent and training.

During the same period, two other Germans, Max von Pettenkoffer and Karl von Voit, conducted a series of elegantly simple experiments that proved to be the first step in exposing the myth of meat. The new science of nutrition had by this time also established that all protein contains nitrogen, which is excreted in urine after protein has been broken down. Knowing this, von Pettenkoffer and Voit were able to determine how much protein was used during athletic competition. They simply collected urine samples from athletes before and immediately after competition and measured the nitrogen content of the samples. Assuming that athletes burned muscle protein during competition, they expected to find more nitrogen in the urine collected after competition. What they discovered, however, was that strenuous activity did not increase nitrogen excretion at all. The conclusion was inescapable: if athletes excrete the same amount of nitrogen before and after exercise, *exercise does not burn protein*, neither muscle protein nor dietary protein. At the very least, the ergogenic value of protein was being exaggerated and the role of protein misunderstood. It took years of research by other investigators to set the record straight.

The word *protein* is derived from ancient Greek words meaning "to take first place." Protein is indeed the paramount nutrient. Half the dry weight of the human body is protein. It is a component of every cell and provides the framework of bones and teeth. There is hardly a physical or chemical process in the body that does not require protein. It is essential for the growth of hair and nails and for the replacement and building of muscle tissue. Protein is vital for these reasons. And protein is vital in the diet, on a regular basis, because the body cannot store it efficiently. As will be seen, the important question for an active athlete is not how much protein to eat but how often to eat it.

Once the true role of protein had been established, the important questions became, How much do people need, and where should they obtain it? In the United States, this line of research began with W. O. Atwater, who discovered that every food has a specific energy value (the calorie later became the standard unit of measurement) and that animals and humans have measurable food-energy requirements. Congress, impressed with the potential of Atwater's work, appropriated funds in 1894 to establish the Department of Agriculture. With Atwater as its first director, the department set out to establish the nutritional needs of the average American.

To establish protein requirements, volunteers were put on a protein-free diet, and their urinary nitrogen output was measured. To this amount was added a small allowance for nitrogen lost through the skin. A much larger allowance was then added to cover the range of individual nutritional requirements. These tests have been refined, and the resulting recommendations have been revised a number of times. The most recent findings show that 98 percent of the adult population — and that includes 98 percent of all athletes — need no more than .37 gram of protein per pound of body weight per day. Growing children and teenagers, pregnant women, and nursing mothers need slightly more.

The .37-gram figure takes into account two other research findings: not all protein eaten is actually used as protein, and some foods have more usable protein than other foods. The reason involves the building blocks of protein: amino acids.

There are hundreds of proteins. Each is a different combination of amino acids. So far, twenty-three amino acids used by the human body have been identified, all but eight of which can be manufactured by the body itself. These eight, called essential amino acids, must come from food, and they must come *at the same time and in a specific ratio.* Fortunately, the essential amino acids are present in almost every source of animal and vegetable protein. Less fortunately, they're never in the exact ratio the body requires. How close the ratio is to the ideal determines how much of the protein can be used. The protein in eggs is closest: over 90 percent can be used. Dairy products, fish, meat, and poultry are also high on the list, with 60–80 percent of their protein usable. Most legumes, grains, and vegetables are lower in usable protein, usually 40–60 percent.

At first, the usability factor misled nutritionists. It continues to mislead the general public, who considers protein from animal sources higher in quality than vegetable protein. These assumptions date to animal experiments performed in the early 1900s by two American researchers, Thomas Osborne and L. B. Mendel. They fed rats various diets, each diet consisting of a single protein-containing food. If the rats fared well, as the ones on animal protein did, the protein was labeled complete. If the rats fared less well, as the ones on grains and vegetables did, the protein was labeled incomplete.

The concept of complete protein is still being promoted by the suppliers of such protein sources. But nutritionists soon realized that this description was inaccurate in several ways. First, the usable portion of incomplete proteins is chemically identical to the usable portion of complete proteins. We simply have to eat more of the incomplete proteins to get the same amount of usable protein. A more important point has been suggested by cross-cultural studies. Americans — on a supposedly superior diet, one high in animal protein — are in no better health than peoples getting their protein largely from "inferior" (vegetable) sources.

The reason is straightforward. In our stomachs, the individual foods we eat are quickly rendered into a rather homogenous porridgelike mass called chyme. What is important nutritionally is the amino acid balance in the chyme. Many vegetables, when eaten in combination, complete one another's amino acid deficiencies. Their protein is then as usable as protein from animal sources. This is known as the principle of the complementarity of proteins, and virtually every ethnic cuisine features complementary protein dishes: rice and beans, tortillas and refried beans, pasta and cheese, cereal and milk, even that old standby, the peanut butter sandwich. Such combinations raise the usability of vegetable protein by 33–50 percent. Researchers have also found that even a very small amount of animal protein in a meal dramatically increases the usability of the meal's vegetable protein. This is the secret of Oriental cuisines, in which vegetables are "garnished" with tiny bits of fish, egg, or meat.

The concept of complementary proteins explains why athletes who are strict vegetarians, like basketball's Bill Walton, or ovo-lacto vegetarians, like tennis star Chris Evert Lloyd and strongman Bill Pearl, never have to worry about getting adequate protein. In fact, when caloric intake is adequate, it is hard to find a diet any-where in the world that is inadequate in protein. It is almost as hard to deliberately design such a diet (unless it is foolishly re-stricted to only a few foods, as is the Beverly Hills diet that was in vogue in 1981). The usability of the protein in any diet con-taining even a modest amount of protein from animal sources — fish, meat, poultry, eggs, milk, and dairy products — is at least 75 percent.

How Much Protein Does an Athlete Need?

If .37 gram per pound is the figure for a normally active adult, what is the figure for *you*, an extremely active athlete? Surely, you might think, you need more protein because you're training and playing hard.

There are indeed certain times when you need extra protein: during the severe stress caused by an accident or illness, for ex-ample, or following heavy physical work. But the extra amount is so inconsequential that you shouldn't give it a second thought.

First, you are already getting more nutrients from the food you eat than your inactive friends do because exercise improves diges-tion. Second, you need more calories when you're working out hard just to maintain your body weight. Unless you choose to get those calories strictly from sugar and fat, you'll get more than enough extra protein simply by eating more food. Finally, you're probably already getting at least 50 percent more meat protein than you need, since the average American diet exceeds the RDA for pro-tein by a full 100 percent.

Nevertheless, it's hard to persuade anyone who wants to build muscle that extra protein is unnecessary. Doesn't muscle building break down more muscle than normal activity? It does, although the exact mechanisms of breaking down and building up are im-perfectly understood. Yet one thing should be understood by any-one who is building muscle: training is progressive. Train too hard and too fast, and you don't build muscle and strength — you lose

53

The Bigger the Better

This bit of tribal wisdom must have originated with the source that gave us "You are what you eat." It underlies another durable sports myth: that bigger muscles are better muscles.

Only bodybuilders like Austrian Oak Arnold Schwarzenegger strive for maximum muscle size for its own sake. A handful of athletes, notably football linebackers, power-lifters, and shot-putters, do need heavy, muscular bodies to perform well. In brief bursts of strength, these athletes use the momentum of a large mass — themselves — to move a heavy object — an opposing player, a barbell, a shot — through space. Simple physics says that the larger the mass, the more easily the object can be moved. Unless you are one of the above kinds of athlete, too much muscle will be detrimental to peak performance.

Study any serious athlete's training regimen and you will find three principal components: (1) general conditioning for endurance and overall fitness, (2) skill-training so as to be better able to meet the technical demands of the sport, and (3) muscle building, but only when required by skill-training. (Of course, progressive-resistance workouts can be a useful component in a general conditioning program.)

Eric Heiden needs massive, overdeveloped thighs for his skating and cycling. He doesn't need an upper torso or arms of proportionate size; the added weight would only slow him down. The converse is true of Kurt Thomas, who needs superbly muscled arms to propel him through his gymnastic routines. He doesn't need legs like Eric Heiden's. So it's no surprise that he hasn't put the same effort into building his thighs that he's spent on building his biceps.

Extra muscle, when it's not required by the demands of your sport, has the same effects on your performance as extra fat: it saps your energy and slows you down. So, before you begin a muscle-building program, consider whether it will help — or hinder.

ground. The question is, In optimal training, how much muscle can be added in any one workout? The answer is, Very little. Even the most dedicated bodybuilders are happy to pack on 10 pounds of muscle in a year. This translates into .03 pound per day. But muscles are only 22 percent protein (the rest is water); so the actual amount of extra protein is only a few grams a day. Such an amount is easily obtained — impossible to avoid, in fact — from the 1000–2000 extra calories that serious bodybuilders must consume to fuel their training. Any additional protein is a waste, and an expensive one. It cannot be used to build muscle. And, as sports nutrition has discovered, it shouldn't be consumed to try to accomplish anything else.

Despite the earlier warning to beware of personal testimonials, no matter how sincere, an unusual report on the dietary value of protein is worthy of mention. It comes from Dr. Ellington Darden, a former athlete and the 1972 NCAA Mr. America, who is now a professional nutritionist, the director of research for the Nautilus Sports Medicine Industries and the author of two diet books. In *Nutrition and Athletic Performance*, he says:

> For ten years, from 1959 to 1969, I was a firm believer in high protein supplements and vitamin pills, as well as various other so-called health foods. I took B-12 for endurance, wheatgerm oil for energy, garlic for purifying the blood, kelp tablets for muscle definition, and vitamin B-6 for strength . . . mainly because I was convinced that the quickest way to become a superior athlete was to follow such a program of eating . . . The majority of [my beliefs] came from popular physical fitness and health magazines. According to these periodicals, most of the recent champions followed such programs. It was not unusual to read a testimonial that a certain diet was at least 75 percent responsible for a winner's victory.

No diet matters that much, and none of the supplements mentioned above can do what athlete Darden had hoped. However, scientist Darden did find that protein was clearly *counter*productive.

After Darden earned his Ph.D., he decided to test the claims made for protein with a series of experiments. He conducted them in the laboratory he knew best: his own body. Over a period of several months, he kept precise records of his caloric intake, including that from protein supplements. At the time, he weighed 215 pounds; so his RDA for protein was 80 grams. But he deliberately varied his intake from less than 100 grams to more than 380 grams per day. He discovered that whenever he consumed more than 100 grams of protein per day that excess was simply excreted.

Significantly, Darden's body weight remained stable throughout the test period, an indication that the excess protein had not built extra muscle. In addition, Darden detected no difference in strength or stamina on days when his protein intake soared. On the other hand, he did notice an appreciable surge of energy when he stopped taking the protein supplements. Thus, he discovered in his personal laboratory that excess protein had at least one definite drawback. Fortunately for him, he did not discover its dangers.

The Perils of Protein

Evidence that protein in excess of the RDA can be harmful has been mounting since the early 1900s. An American scientist, Russell Chittenden, demonstrated that the excretion of the excess nitrogen that accumulates during periods of extremely high protein intake puts a strain on the kidneys. In anyone whose kidney function is already impaired, this strain can lead to further kidney damage.

It soon became clear that other health problems associated with a diet high in animal protein are even more serious. Meat, especially beef and pork, is extremely high in fat. The dry weight of a T-bone steak, for example, is 80 percent fat. Fat plays an essential role in human nutrition (see chapter 6). It also plays a far less welcome role in cardiovascular disease and obesity. As with protein, enough fat is enough, more is harmful, and most Americans are getting twice as much as they need.

A high-protein, high-fat diet is also associated with a higher risk of colon cancer. The National Institute of Aging strongly suspects that excess protein accelerates the aging process, probably because of the additional stress it places on metabolism. In addition, a Columbia University research team has discovered that protein supplements taken during pregnancy reduce birth weight, and low birth weight is the most significant factor in infant mortality. And researchers have found that a high-protein diet can cause the body to deplete its reserves of various minerals. In the case of calcium, the depletion can lead to osteoporosis, the brittle-bone syndrome that afflicts the elderly. As if all these long-range health problems weren't enough, there is now a growing conviction among sports nutritionists that a high-protein diet can very quickly impair performance.

For most athletes, a high-protein diet comes not at the expense of fats but at the expense of carbohydrates. Yet it is carbohydrates that are the active body's principal source of energy. Armed with this knowledge, some elite endurance athletes deliberately deny themselves carbohydrates as a preliminary step in a carbohydrate-loading program. They report that the initial low-carbohydrate, high-fat, high-protein phase reduces their endurance dramatically. The Swedish sports scientists who originated this type of diet found that the drop in endurance could be as high as 50 percent.

More evidence against high-protein diets is coming from researchers on the front lines in the battle of the bulge. The word is that a high-protein diet is not only the wrong way to try to build muscle; it's also the wrong way to try to lose weight.

If you have ever had a weight problem, you're probably familiar with the high-protein, low-carbohydrate diet under one or more of its various names: Scarsdale, Stillman, Atkins, Air Force, Drinking Man's, Calories Don't Count, or the "Mayo" (which has no connection whatsoever with the clinic of the same name). These diets differ superficially, but they're all basically the same. Even when they are billed as revolutionary, there is nothing revolutionary or new about them. They are nothing more than warmed-over versions of a diet plan that was devised more than a century ago and was known in Victorian England as the Banting diet, in honor of its inventor, Dr. William Banting.

For reasons that were not clearly understood at the time, Banting's diet, which was high in protein and extremely low in both complex and simple carbohydrates, produced rapid weight loss. In an age of nine-course meals and overample figures, it proved extremely popular, and soon half the fashionable women of London were "Banting" between bouts of overeating.

Today, the mechanics of the diet are understood, and the consequences of this radically unbalanced regimen are such that it should never be considered by any athlete. A high-protein, low-carbohydrate diet forces the body to burn dietary fat and protein for energy and, if the caloric intake is low enough, stored fat and muscle protein as well. Burning stored fat is almost as efficient as burning carbohydrates, but the process produces by-products called ketones. The only good thing that can be said about ketones is that they are a mild appetite suppressant. In the blood, however, ketones produce an acid imbalance, which, in the large amounts associated with a high-fat diet, can eventually lower blood pressure and even lead to a condition much like diabetes.

Forcing the body to burn protein for energy has even more unwelcome side effects. It's a little like throwing unseasoned, green wood on a fire. Only about half the calories of protein can be converted to energy. In the process, potentially harmful by-products, such as ammonia, are produced. To dilute these toxins, the body draws upon its water stores, using seven times more water to burn protein than fat or carbohydrates. The toxins are then excreted through the kidneys in copious amounts of urine. This water loss accounts for the initial, rapid weight loss associated with high-protein diets. The weight loss is an illusion, of course. The dieter is simply dehydrated. When normal eating and drinking habits are resumed, the body rehydrates, and body weight returns to its former level.

It is the *apparent* effectiveness of high-protein diets that accounts for their enormous popularity — and condemns those who try them to a cycle of trying and failing. No athlete would knowingly put such a strain on his or her body or mind. No athlete can afford a diet that is dehydrating. Even if you are intent on building muscle rather than losing weight, the message should be clear: a diet high in animal protein — and therefore unavoidably high in fat — can put you in jeopardy. Hoping to build muscle, you may only erode your endurance by neglecting the carbohydrates that are your ideal source of energy. Like Dr. Darden, you may experience one or more of the recognized side effects of a high-protein, low-carbohydrate regimen: fatigue, headache, constipation, tension, and irritability.

Rather than worry about getting enough protein, you would more profitably wonder if you're getting too much. The average American diet contains an overabundance of protein, and there are many indications that less protein represents a more balanced diet.

Laboratory animals on low-protein diets, for instance, are more, not less, resistant to stress, fatigue, infection, and injury than are ones on high-protein diets. Patients with high blood pressure or heart, artery, or kidney disease benefit from diets that contain roughly half the normal RDA. Cross-cultural studies have revealed societies on every continent that subsist on low-protein diets and are remarkably fit, healthy, and durable.

Despite the evidence that favors low-protein diets and warns against high-protein diets, the surplus you're getting probably falls within the range of excess that your body can handle without untoward consequences. But it definitely isn't helping you. As with all other nutrients, extra protein is not a form of insurance. It's a waste.

What is worth your concern is how often you eat protein. Protein is not efficiently stored by the body, and reserves begin to decline after about three hours. So you should include protein in every meal. There's no evidence that getting it more often than this is better, but if you eat a small amount at each of three meals and at as many snacks, you will guarantee yourself optimal reserves at all times. If you choose to get your protein this often, however, keep in mind how little you will need at any one time. Bran cereal and milk, a container of yogurt, a peanut butter sandwich, a glass of milk, half a small can of tuna, the smallest fast food hamburger — the protein in these six items exceeds your RDA unless you weigh over 200 pounds. That's how easy it is to get more than enough protein.

* * *

To summarize, despite the hardy myth of meat, it doesn't matter where you get your protein. In combination, vegetable protein is as usable as animal protein. The problem with meat, however, is not its protein but the fat. This is the reason you should consider eating less meat and switching to low-fat dairy products.

Protein *is* essential, but it doesn't increase strength. Exercise does. Strenuous exercise requires very little extra protein. There is no advantage in exceeding your RDA, and doing so has some definite drawbacks, such as forcing your body to burn protein for energy. So stop thinking of extra protein as insurance, especially if it's in the form of protein supplements. They are an expensive way to add protein to a diet that already oversupplies the nutrient.

6

Fuels for the Inner Fire

Athletes are forever looking for more energy.

WALTER H. GREGG
Chairman, Health and Physical Education
Northwestern University

ASLEEP OR AWAKE, in training or during off-season, at idle or full throttle, we burn energy all the time. But we don't take in energy at the same rate as we expend it. Bridging the gap between these two rates is a remarkably flexible system of energy storage and utilization. This system is so flexible, in fact, that our bodies will store and burn almost anything we eat. They do have preferences, however, and athletes who respect these preferences gain an important competitive advantage in both the short and long runs. Gaining this advantage starts with understanding how our bodies turns food into fuel.

From Food to Fuel

The main sources of energy in food are fats and carbohydrates. Protein is a less efficient, secondary energy source. Vitamins and minerals are not sources of energy, but they do play indirect, supporting roles in the use of energy. In the digestive system, fats, carbohydrates, and protein are broken into their components, which are absorbed into the bloodstream.

Fats (lipids) enter the bloodstream as fatty acids and glycerol. They can be stored, temporarily or indefinitely, in fat cells located throughout the body. Fatty acids, whether they have come directly

60

from the digestive system or have been released by fat cells, are used as fuel by cells in all parts of the body except the brain and nerves. The liver uses glycerol, as well as excess glucose and amino acids, to produce fat, which can then be stored. Therefore, one training goal is to maintain adequate but not excessive fat reserves.

Carbohydrates, which are complex chains of sugars, enter the bloodstream as the simplest sugar, glucose. Two-thirds of this glucose is stored in the liver as glycogen. This glycogen is easily converted back to glucose, which the liver doles out to meet the steady and unvarying energy needs of the brain and nervous system. When the liver depletes its glycogen supply, it can make glucose from amino acids or ketones from fatty acids, and the brain and nerves will use the glucose or ketones for fuel. These alternatives produce energy less efficiently, however. Most glucose that is not stored in the liver is stored in the muscles as glycogen. This glycogen is the primary fuel of hardworking muscles and can be used only by muscles. It cannot be released into the bloodstream as glucose. Glycogen reserves last two to twelve hours, depending on a person's level of physical activity. When the muscles run out of glycogen, they can shift gears and burn fatty acids or glucose. Because this is somewhat less efficient, another training goal is to increase the reserves of muscle glycogen.

Protein enters the bloodstream as amino acids. They are used by the muscles and other cells for maintenance, repair, and growth. Excess amino acids that are not needed by these cells can be converted to fat by the liver. Or, if the liver is out of glycogen, it can convert amino acids to glucose in order to keep the brain and nerves supplied with fuel. These alternatives also produce energy less efficiently. Therefore, a third training goal is to meet the body's protein needs but not at the expense of its glycogen needs (see chapter 5).

Fuel Consumption

The entire process described above continuously balances the body's moment-to-moment energy needs, the amount of fuel entering the body from food, and the amount of fuel stored in its cells. It's remarkable how long and how well the survival-oriented body will perform when it is denied an optimal mix of fuels, or denied fuel altogether. But it's a far cry from how the body will perform when the mix is right. The right mix — an optimal diet — is only one aspect of fuel consumption, however. There are other aspects that must be considered too.

Diet. Few of us need to be reminded how easy it is to increase our fat reserves. But we can also increase our glycogen reserves, the primary fuel of hardworking muscles and the first one that active athletes run out of. If we switch to a diet that is higher in carbohydrates but no higher in calories, our weight won't be affected. Our glycogen stores, on the other hand, will be. As a result our bodies will not have to switch to alternate but less efficient performance fuels as soon as they would have to otherwise. In fact, they might not have to make the switch at all.

Effort. At rest, we burn fat in the form of fatty acids. At peak effort, we burn carbohydrates in the form of glycogen. In between, we mix the two fuels. Ordinarily, glycogen supplies aren't depleted rapidly, but during continuous physical activity, they can be depleted in as little as two hours. This is why endurance athletes are interested in anything that will increase glycogen stores or conserve glycogen by tipping the fat–glycogen mix towards fat. So far, the only glycogen-sparing substance that has been found is caffeine (see chapter 11). But even nonendurance athletes reach a point at which they run out of muscle glycogen and then liver glycogen.

What the transition to other fuels feels like depends primarily on what is being done at the time. If the activity is one that requires little effort, there is a sense of fatigue; if moderate effort, a zone of discomfort; if great effort, what marathoners call hitting the wall.

Fitness. One key measure of fitness is the efficiency of the lungs, heart, and arteries in transporting oxygen, without which fuel won't "burn." The more efficient the transportation — that is, the better trained the body — the more efficiently the fuel will be used. Training also increases the body's ability to store glycogen. In addition, if the body is forced to switch to other fuels during practice or competition, training enables the switch to be made more easily.

Wherever we fall on the continuum that separates the armchair athlete from the world-class athlete in intensive training, we all

ATP

Our bodies are sometimes compared to internal combustion engines, which burn fuel and oxygen to produce energy. This comparison is useful but also oversimplified. The human body is far more sophisticated than any engine, and it uses fuel in a complex process that is affected by various enzymes, vitamins, and minerals.

Within our cells, oxygen doesn't burn with fuel. It reacts with fuel — glucose and fatty acids — to produce simpler compounds, the most important of which is adenosine triphosphate (ATP). ATP is the main source of energy for muscular work. It can release its energy instantly and without oxygen, enabling us to function without being directly dependent on our oxygen supply. ATP is the reason why we can produce a tremendous burst of strength or speed — cleaning and jerking a barbell or running the 50-yard dash — without taking a breath.

Unless we replenish our oxygen supply, of course, we'd soon keel over. We need it to form new ATP, which would otherwise be exhausted in about two minutes. And the same red blood cells that deliver oxygen remove the carbon dioxide that results from oxygen's reaction with glucose and fatty acids. So even though oxygen doesn't "burn" fuel, it is essential to the energy-production process, and an important performance factor in any effort lasting more than a couple of minutes. This is why cardiovascular efficiency — the body's ability to deliver oxygen to the muscles — is the key measure of fitness. And this is why exercise plans that are aerobic (literally, "with air"), increase cardiovascular efficiency and thereby improve our endurance.

take in, store, and burn fuel the same way. And the basic considerations regarding fats and carbohydrates in the diet and in the body are the same for all of us.

Fat

Fat *is* functional, but its functions have been obscured. In an age of central heating and down jackets, the fact that fat insulates us may not seem very important, especially when a layer of fat weighs so much more than a layer of down. Fat also cushions and protects us, though a lot of athletic equipment does that just as well if not better.

The role of fat in growth and health is far more essential. Our cells need fat to repair and replace themselves, not just for energy. Fat is also necessary for the absorption and storage of the fat-soluble vitamins, A, D, E, and K. Finally, about 80 percent of our energy reserves are in the form of fat. And it's good that they are. One gram of fat yields 9 calories of energy, more than twice that of an equivalent amount of protein or carbohydrate. To put this another way, body fat — pound for pound — contains twice as much stored energy as muscle glycogen. Only under the demands of hard physical work does glycogen burn better than fat. This is why it is preferred by hardworking muscles. But if all our energy reserves were in the form of glycogen, the extra weight would be an unacceptable burden.

Biologically, body fat is an entirely praiseworthy product of evolution: it is the body's primary tool for balancing the input of food and the output of energy. But the importance of this was more obvious when the food supply was unpredictable and the time between meals was as likely to be days as hours. Life was (and in some societies, still is) a permanent cycle of feast or famine. Without the ability to store energy efficiently, humans simply wouldn't have survived. It is small wonder, then, that among the earliest artifacts of civilization are depictions of extraordinarily full-figured women. These fertility symbols suggest the crucial role that body fat has played in human survival. In early times, only the hardiest women — those with ample energy reserves — survived the demands of childbirth and nursing. These rigors toughened the species. That they also promoted the survival of the fattest was never apparent until societies like ours were able to produce so predictable and overabundant a food supply.

Today, a goodly number of us must struggle with our bodies' innate capacity for storing fat. The mechanism that once promoted survival now interferes with it, directly in the form of obesity and indirectly as a contributing factor in heart disease and possibly some kinds of cancer. Of more immediate concern to athletes, excess body fat slows the body down every step of the way.

Body Fat. Assuming you are that rarely encountered creature,

The Other Fat

There are two kinds of body fat. What we usually mean when we talk about body fat is yellow, or white, fat, which represents our energy reserves. Another form of fat, however, is not for burning. It is brown fat, the hard fat between our shoulder blades. It protects, and is a constituent of, our internal organs and major blood vessels, and it's essential to our well-being. Although the amount of brown fat varies from person to person, it's always a small fraction of the total fat — 1 percent or so. Some researchers think it may help control weight by burning energy rather than storing it. This could be one more reason why some people — invariably someone else — seem to be able to eat as much as they want and never gain weight.

the average athlete, your body weight is about 15 percent fat if you're a male and about 20 percent if you're a female (the difference is the biological margin of safety for pregnancy, childbirth, and nursing). Subtract 5 percent and you're on the lean side; add 5 and you're on the heavy side.

Those endurance athletes who are whippet-thin often have bodies that are less than 5 percent fat. During competition, the leanest of them may deplete their fat reserves completely. (As a result, they begin burning muscle for fuel, and the evidence is visible in their urine, which is dark from the by-products of protein combustion.) Wrestlers, gymnasts, dancers, even many of the hulks encountered in football, weightlifting, and bodybuilding are often less than 15 percent body fat. At this level, dancers, gymnasts, and bodybuilders have the aesthetic look they want, and wrestlers and other weight-class athletes have more power per pound.

What firsthand experience has taught such athletes, sports science has confirmed: performance is closely related to body composition — that is, to the ratio of fat to lean. The simple fact is that most of us, with the exception of marathon swimmers and sumo wrestlers, have a lot more fat than we'll ever need. But does an ultralow amount of body fat offer regular athletes the same ergogenic advantages it offers champions? Not necessarily.

Leanness in elite athletes is primarily the result of intensive training. They actually lose body fat on diets that may have 100 percent more calories than most of us routinely eat. This high caloric intake protects their health and energy by providing an abundant and steady supply of nutrients.

Such is not the case with hardworking athletes who have a habit of crash-dieting, fasting, or sweating off excess pounds to "make weight." High-school and college wrestlers who engage in these practices have been the subjects of some medical concern and several studies. Because these athletes are young and physically resilient, they usually experience only a slight, short-term reduction in strength. Nevertheless, the American Medical Association's Committee on the Medical Aspects of Sports has been concerned enough to label these drastic approaches hazardous. It recommends that all young wrestlers meet minimum body-fat standards and suggests 7–10 percent as a guideline.

A problem sometimes experienced by ultralean female athletes is amenorrhea, a cessation of menstruation. When body fat is less than 20 percent or so, one of every three women experiences irregular menstrual cycles or stops ovulating altogether. This is the body's protective response to a caloric deficit. Until recently, low body fat meant a low chance of surviving the demands of pregnancy, childbirth, and nursing. Nature protects undernourished women by interrupting their fertility cycles. Because hardworking female athletes *are* eating enough to meet all their nutritional requirements, however, amenorrhea is not considered a health problem for them. Indeed, this is only one of many ways in which superbly conditioned athletes can confound the medical norms for good health.

For most of us, decreasing our body fat to almost nothing is not a realistic or desirable goal, because we cannot devote the time and energy it takes to be both lean and healthy. A more meaningful issue is whether we are satisfied with the size of the person we see in the mirror. Far too much is made in our society of what is, in fact, only a few extra pounds. Optimal weight is relative. Optimal for what and for whom? Consult the chart in chapter 4 to find your "ideal" weight. But keep this in mind: statistics show that weight can be as much as 10 percent more or less than "ideal" weight without posing any known health risk. Even additional weight is less of a problem than the endless cycle of weight loss

Too Rich, Too Thin

Fashion-conscious people who follow the dictum that it is impossible to be too rich or too thin are only half right. When the pursuit of thinness is based on a severely restricted diet, health problems more serious than those associated with being overweight can result. At the very least, a Park Avenue socialite can't possibly feel her best on a daily diet of 1000 calories or less. She may take a pill to compensate for the vitamins and minerals she's missing. But it will do nothing for her lack of energy, because vitamins and minerals — no matter how we obtain them — have no calories. And without adequate fuel, forget about adequate energy.

If you want minimum body fat and maximum energy but can't make the training commitment of an elite athlete, you face a tough diet–training challenge. First, you must protect your glycogen reserves with a high-carbohydrate diet. Then you must make every calorie count *without* counting calories. (If your energy sags, you're not eating enough, and you're losing weight too fast.)

These are the basic principles of the Intensive Training diet described in detail in chapter 12. In essence, it's a near-vegetarian diet that emphasizes grains and grain products, vegetables, and fruits; eliminates sugar; and drastically restricts fats. It's the healthiest low-calorie diet you can follow. But it's dramatically different from the way you're eating now. The Eat-to-Win plan presented in chapter 12 can also help you lose body fat. It will improve your eating patterns without dramatically changing them, and it may be all you need to reach your desired weight.

and weight gain that characterizes the American approach to dieting. Still, obesity — 35 percent or more over "ideal" weight — is one of our leading health problems, and there is no doubt that excess fat in our bodies is directly related to excess fat in our diets, and to lack of exercise.

Dietary Fat. Dietary fat and body fat are not necessarily the same thing. And just because most of what we burn for fuel is fat doesn't mean that most of what we eat should be fat. In truth, however, we're uncomfortably close to this fat-to-fat equation. Forty-two percent of the average American diet is fat; only the West German diet contains more. As a nation, we consume over ten *billion* pounds of fats and oils (which are liquid fats) each year. For the average adult male, this works out to more than 150 grams — 1350 calories — of fat per day. One thing that all health officials agree on is that this is far too much fat.

The drawbacks of a high-fat diet begin with the fact that our bodies can and do manufacture fat from anything we eat. Fat, having over twice as many calories per gram as carbohydrates and protein do, just fattens us faster. High-fat diets are also a prime contributor to heart disease, which is epidemic in this country. Some researchers are especially worried about the saturated fats (fats from animal sources) in our diets. Unlike unsaturated fats from vegetable sources, saturated fats contain cholesterol, and high levels of cholesterol in the blood are associated with a high risk of heart disease. There is almost universal agreement that lowering our total intake of fats is the most sensible single step we can take to protect ourselves from a host of health problems, ranging from obesity, which itself contributes to other problems, to heart disease and possibly even some forms of cancer.

High-fat diets are almost always low-carbohydrate diets, a serious concern for athletes interested in maintaining or increasing their glycogen stores without gaining weight. High-fat meals also slow the passage of food from the stomach into the intestines. This matters most when we need to get high-performance fuels out of our stomachs and into our systems as quickly as possible: before training and competition.

Because of these day-in, day-out disadvantages of a high-fat diet, most professional training camps have broken the steak habit and are now encouraging their players to tank up on carbohydrates in the form of grain products, fruits, and vegetables. These foods leave the stomach faster, and they provide hardworking athletes with the muscle energy that is their prime requirement.

If a high-fat diet is not optimal, how much fat is? That's a debatable question with no clear-cut medical answer. Almost all nutritionists advise that we reduce the fat content of our diets to around 30 percent. The Japanese, however, with far less obesity and heart disease than we have, average about 20 percent. Octogenarians in Pakistan, Ecuador, and Soviet Georgia, still working hard and eating less than 2000 calories a day, have diets that range from 25 percent to as little as 12 percent fat — about one-third to one-tenth the amount of total dietary fat that we get.

Though fats are essential to growth and health, there are no commonly accepted minimum daily requirements. Only in the laboratory is it possible to design a calorically adequate diet so low in fat that the health problems associated with fat deprivation become readily apparent. Even if we were scrupulously to avoid adding any fat to the foods we eat, keep our meat consumption to a minimum, use only low-fat milk and dairy products, and avoid nuts, seeds, and other naturally high-fat foods like the avocado, our diets would still be about 10 percent fat. No one has demonstrated that a regimen this low in fat is risky, although some nutritionists worry that, in the long run, it may shortchange us of the fatty acids that we do need and make it more difficult to meet our needs for vitamins A, D, E, and K, which depend on dietary fat to be absorbed into the system.

A reasonable conclusion is that dietary fat is the one essential component of nutrition that we can most drastically reduce with the greatest safety. Another conclusion is that, for most of us, the issue of dietary fat ranks with the issue of body fat: it takes so much work to wind up with too little fat that it's not worth worrying about. A diet that is ultralow in fat requires tremendous determination and dramatic changes in eating patterns. Such a diet is almost certainly healthful (as long as it is calorically adequate), but it is definitely impractical and probably unnecessary.

The Law of Diminishing Returns. One wonderful thing about getting involved in athletics is that an improvement in fitness, appearance, and performance is quickly noticeable. For example, twenty minutes of steady running at a moderate pace three times a week provides most of the cardiovascular benefits of the most intensive training. Athletes in intensive training, however, inevitably encounter the law of diminishing returns. Greater and greater effort is necessary for progressively smaller improvements: a tenth-of-a-second increase in speed, an extra pound of muscle, a hundredth-of-a-point higher score.

It would be great to be able to announce the discovery of a point of diminishing returns when it comes to dietary fat — a point beyond which the benefits don't justify the effort. There probably is one, but where it is has not been found. Still, no one defends a diet that is 42 percent fat, and hardly anyone except an Ecuadorian octogenarian finds 12 percent any more desirable. Twenty percent was settled on for the Eat-to-Win Basic Training plan for two reasons. It's the figure most often mentioned by nutritionists that is known to meet our need for fatty acids and fat-soluble vitamins comfortably. It's also a somewhat challenging, but entirely realistic, dietary goal.

But don't interpret the 20 percent figure as some sort of rule or absolute. There are too many of those around as it is. Nutritional measurements are essential for nutritionists. Yet they have a way of distracting the rest of us from the real issue: our overall eating patterns and how they affect the way we feel and perform. Twenty percent is meaningful only if you can internalize it and put it to work as a kind of mental marker to help you recognize and evaluate the evidence of your own senses. You can see fat on your body, and you can learn to see it in your food. You'll find out how in chapter 12.

Carbohydrates

Although fat is the primary source of energy in light to moderate activity, it is nevertheless a secondary muscle fuel. And because most of us, even those of us who are thin, have such abundant fat reserves, running out is rarely a realistic concern. The same cannot be said about glycogen — our stored reserves of carbohydrates.

Only a small percentage of our total energy reserves is in the form of glycogen. Why, then, is it the main muscle fuel? For one reason, glycogen is stored *in* the muscle, where it is immediately available. For another, under conditions of intense activity, glycogen and oxygen burn twice as efficiently as fat and oxygen.

In theory, if you were to make an all-out isometric effort against an immovable object, you could deplete the muscles you used of glycogen in only a few minutes. But long before that moment arrived, you would have collapsed from exhaustion. In practice, the lower limits of glycogen depletion have been most thoroughly explored by marathon runners. After about two hours of running at 85–90 percent of their maximum effort, they experience a rapid onset of pain, fatigue, and weakness, a syndrome best described by the name they have given it: hitting the wall.

The wall is a high-intensity phenomenon, which is why most of us, if we do manage to reach it, hardly notice it. Count your blessings, say some elite runners, while others swear that the wall is more myth than reality. There are points of exhaustion in every sport, the latter say, and if you don't reach one along the way, then you aren't trying your hardest. The impact of the wall, they add, has also been exaggerated. There is a zone of difficulty, true, but it doesn't hit you like a wall.

In researching the reality behind the wall, sports scientists have found both arguments to be accurate. Individual differences affect our reactions to everything, the wall included. But experienced endurance athletes do have an advantage — their experience. By repeatedly depleting their muscle glycogen during practice, they train their bodies to make the transition from burning glycogen to burning fat and glucose more efficiently — so much more so that an experienced marathoner is as much as 700 percent better at it than a beginner.

Research into glycogen depletion has uncovered another benefit: depletion enhances storage. The storage process is regulated by enzymes that balance glycogen stores with activity levels. Any increase in activity signals the enzymes to increase the body's glycogen stores. This process works best when muscle glycogen is completely depleted before refueling.

The realization that depletion can significantly enhance glycogen reserves led to the development of what is still a controversial technique for boosting glycogen stores. It is commonly called carbohydrate loading, but it is, more accurately, a glycogen-depletion–glycogen-loading program designed by sports scientists in Sweden in the mid-1960s. They found that a specific sequence of diet-and-exercise steps could increase glycogen stores and that the extra glycogen translated into greater endurance in the athletes they were studying.

The technique works this way: Seven days before competition, you do a long workout designed to deplete your glycogen stores. Then, rather than refueling with a high-carbohydrate meal, you studiously avoid carbohydrates in favor of protein and fats for the next three days, while you continue your training. This dietary change primes the enzymes in your muscles, leaving them so eager for glycogen that they will absorb all you can give them. The following three days, you eat a high-carbohydrate diet. By starting time, your muscles are supercharged with glycogen, and the dreaded wall is farther down the road than it would have been.

All this sounds good. But strict carbohydrate loading has a definite disadvantage that has limited its acceptance even among top endurance athletes. The disadvantage is related to the three-day low-carbohydrate phase. The high-protein, high-fat diet eaten at this time is nutritionally unbalanced and unsound. It can affect mood and sleep patterns, and it definitely affects energy levels. None of this is likely to benefit mental attitude, even if the effects are known to be temporary.

Another problem with strict carbohydrate loading is that the enzymes are tricked into exceeding their limits. Eating a bit more or loading a bit faster than normal can result in muscles that are painfully sore from the glycogen overload. Unless some of the surplus glycogen is burned by exercise, thereby defeating the whole process of loading, muscle tissue can actually be ruptured before the athlete ever gets off the mark.

Is the plan worth its potential risks? Elite endurance athletes, who will try almost anything to increase their endurance, are divided on the value of strict carbohydrate loading. This underscores the importance of considering individual differences in all nutritional issues. If you want to try this out-of-the-ordinary nutritional manipulation, give yourself plenty of time to experiment and find the number of low-carbohydrate and high-carbohydrate days that works for you. Or follow the lead of many world-class runners who load continually — without the low-carbohydrate phase. They may be sacrificing a small amount of additional muscle glycogen, but they've decided that maintaining their energy level throughout training is smarter in the long run.

Is carbohydrate loading a meaningful issue for nonendurance athletes? If you don't go all out, or even nearly all out, for two hours or more, your muscle glycogen is probably not the limiting factor in your performance. Your basic level of activity primes the body to store all the glycogen you need, if you give it half a chance. But that may be just what you aren't giving it.

Having adequate glycogen stores depends on an adequate intake of carbohydrates. Only 43 percent of the calories in the average American diet are from carbohydrates — a measly 1 percent more than from fat. The consensus is that this amount is inadequate and, as noted earlier, requires the body to turn to fuels that are less efficient sources of energy for hard work. When the body does this, the loss of efficiency can be felt; more seriously, however, the muscles may be put in competition with the brain.

About ten or fifteen minutes after exercise begins, the liver begins to release extra glucose. This excess is destined not for the brain, whose needs are constant, but for the muscles — as a secondary fuel while they're using glycogen. Once the muscles run out of glycogen, their need for glucose increases. This increase puts extra demands on the liver until it too runs out of glycogen. To keep the brain supplied with fuel — the liver's highest priority — the liver makes glucose from amino acids or ketones from fatty acids. In the interim, the brain responds to the decreasing level of glucose in the bloodstream by sending out strong fatigue and hunger signals.

These signals are strongest in the athletes who have been working the longest and hardest, and they're worse than hitting the wall. Marathoners who have pushed past the wall, for example, are pitting fuel-starved muscles against the brain and the declining resources of the liver. Something has to give. The liver runs out of glycogen, but before it can produce substitutes, the level of glucose in the blood drops dramatically. Starved of fuel, the brain — and the athlete — tend to go a little haywire. Cold sweats, dizziness, loss of coordination, and mental confusion set in. Marathoners call it bonking, because the victims do go bonkers. They may actually think they're running like gazelles and may have to be physically restrained by those who recognize the symptoms.

The only solution to bonking is to stop and eat. Muscles then won't require as much glucose, and digestion, slowed or stopped by intense activity, will return to normal. If the food eaten is high in carbohydrates, glucose will quickly make its way into the system.

Like hitting the wall, bonking is a high-intensity phenomenon. At lesser activity levels, it's felt as fatigue, which is less dramatic but no more desirable. The way to protect yourself against fatigue in any form is to protect and enhance the glycogen stores in your liver before you exercise. Your muscles require extra activity to load extra glycogen, but the level of glycogen in your liver is directly related to the level of carbohydrates in your diet. One day of a carbohydrate-poor diet can completely deplete your liver glycogen. In contrast, one day of a carbohydrate-rich diet can double it.

For most of us, loading liver glycogen is more important than loading muscle glycogen, because at moderate activity levels and with a typical American diet, the liver is more likely than the muscles to come up empty. This means that the brain and central nervous system are deprived of their best fuel reserves. The liver manufactures alternative fuels, of course, but the process is necessary rather than optimal — and the price is unnecessary fatigue.

A high-carbohydrate diet is the best guarantee of ample glycogen reserves, and it usually avoids the problems associated with "fueling up" during competition, which is an almost universal athletic practice but one that is far from universally necessary or productive. Distance swimmers and skiers, ultramarathoners, and cyclists who go for hours must eat or they will run out of liver glycogen — not with high-intensity bonking but with a big drop in energy. For most marathoners who run the race in three hours or less, the bonking point is safely past the finishing line, but slower marathoners may have to run even more slowly and eat something along the way if they want to finish. Actually, that something is often the most misunderstood fuel an athlete can use.

Sugar and the Myth of Quick Energy

We are all born with a built-in preference for naturally sweet foods, a preference that once aided survival by guiding people to the ripe fruits that are important sources of carbohydrate energy, vitamins, and minerals. The sweet tooth worked well for people — until sugar was refined. Since the 1920s, the per capita consumption of sugar in the United States has hovered around one hundred pounds per year. In the past few years, we've been eating less candy and using less household sugar than we had been, but the amount of sugar in processed foods has more than doubled, and our consumption of soft drinks has quadrupled. Over 50 percent of our carbohydrate intake and 25 percent of all our calories are in the form of sugar. Our preference for sweet foods has gone from virtue to vice.

The problem with sugar starts with its irrelevancy. It is the one item in the diet that can be eliminated with absolutely no risk, because the body has absolutely no need for dietary sugar in any

Sugar by Any Other Name . . .

Whether it's called sugar, sucrose, fructose, dextrose, maltose, lactose, corn syrup, or honey, whether it's manufactured by people or by bees, all sugars are essentially the same. Chemically, sugars are the simplest carbohydrates, either monosaccharides or disaccharides. Much is sometimes made of the difference between them, but the digestive system makes short work of the weak chemical bond that keeps table sugar, a disaccharide, from becoming glucose, a monosaccharide.

Nutritionally, refined sugar in all its forms has little going for it except its calories. Fructose, one of the sugars found in fruits, is currently being hyped because it is somewhat sweeter than sugar. But the caloric saving in substituting fructose for sugar is inconsequential, while the financial cost is considerable. As for honey's healthful reputation, well, it does contain more potassium than sugar. Yet as *Consumer Reports* tartly observes, we would need about ninety tablespoons of honey to meet our potassium requirement.

Whenever someone touts one form of sugar as nutritionally superior, remember the rules of multiplication: anything multiplied by practically nothing equals not very much.

form. It is ideally equipped to obtain all the glucose it needs from naturally occurring carbohydrates in food. Sugar *is* a carbohydrate, but it has no nutritional value except calories. It is for this reason that the term *empty calorie* was coined.

If sugar contributes nothing but empty calories, its main defect would seem to be the burden it places on other calories in the diet to provide even more nutrients. But sugar has other faults. Empty calories can still result in unwanted weight. In addition, sugar is a carbohydrate in such a highly refined form that it actually begins to be digested by bacteria in the mouth. This results in the production of acids, which decay teeth. Tooth decay occurred in only 5 percent of our prehistoric ancestors and 10 percent of the world population until the 1700s. Today, it occurs in 97 percent of Americans.

Few athletes who consume sugar, however, are worried about tooth decay. They expect sugar to live up to its ergogenic reputation as a fatigue fighter and energy booster. It's hard to convince them that, with few exceptions, sugar is *anti*ergogenic.

Here's the problem: We feel tired when our blood glucose level drops. So we consume something with a lot of refined sugar in it, a soft drink or a candy bar, for example. Carbohydrates in any form are the most readily digested and absorbed nutrients. But sugar, which is a simple carbohydrate that is only one insignificant chemical step from being glucose, races into our system. Our blood sugar level jumps, and so does our energy. Before we have a chance to profit from that boost, however, the pancreas goes a bit bananas. Evolution has taught it a lot about complex carbohydrates but little about refined sugar. It judges the jump in blood glucose, assumes a lot more is on the way (as there would be if the glucose were from more slowly digested complex carbohydrates), and releases an extra dose of insulin. Normally, this insulin clears the bloodstream of excess glucose and helps the liver and muscles store it. The extra insulin, however, sweeps so much glucose from the bloodstream that we're left with even less than we had when we started, and with even more fatigue. Some people experience this rebound effect more acutely than others, and they are said to suffer from sugar blues. It's hardly a dreaded disease, but it can impair athletic performance. Happily, it's easily avoided by avoiding so-called high-energy foods that are high in sugar.

Sugar may be antiergogenic in normal circumstances, but the conditions of competition are often abnormal. During intense, sustained activity, the only nutritional issue of any immediate importance is energy. The fact that sugar contains a quickly digested form of energy then matters much more than its lack of other nutrients. This is why sports scientists have done a lot of experimenting with sugar intake during and just before exercise.

These researchers have found that at low and moderate activity levels, glucose (the form of sugar that is usually administered in such studies) does have a counterproductive, rebound effect. Only when effort is exerted at high intensity for two hours or more does glucose intake during exercise have a positive impact on endurance by helping the liver conserve glycogen. Yet even then, the impact of glucose is not always positive. For one thing, intense activity practically stops digestion. Whether marathoners, who operate at 85–90 percent of peak output, can digest anything is almost en-

Demon Sugar?

In some circles, sugar has been equated with evil incarnate. Adelle Davis made much of the fact that the Manson family consumed countless candy bars. And the late J. I. Rodale once wrote an off-Broadway play on the sugar–crime connection. Entitled *The Goose,* it dramatized the efforts of an idealistic young social worker to reform a juvenile delinquent with a serious Coke habit. More recently, it has been suggested that Dan White's motive for assassinating Mayor George Moscone and Supervisor Harvey Milk in San Francisco had less to do with his desire for revenge and hatred of homosexuals than with his overindulgence in Twinkies. There's a lot to be said for cutting your sugar consumption, but nipping your criminal tendencies in the bud isn't one of the advantages.

tirely a matter of individual differences. In addition, the maximum amount of energy they can absorb is limited to about 200 calories per hour. Ultraendurance athletes, operating at 50–70 percent of maximum, can digest food, although digestion is slower than normal and the range of individual differences is still great.

When activity slows digestion, two other problems present themselves. Food, whether it is glucose or something else, sits in the stomach, increasing the chance of stomach upset. Moreover, this food draws fluids from the rest of the body to aid digestion. This can be disastrous. Whenever we're sweating hard, the biggest threat to performance is dehydration, and preserving the fluid reserves in our bodies is far more important than augmenting our energy reserves. (The critical issue of fluid replacement is discussed in detail in the next chapter.)

In practice, those who might benefit from a small amount of sugar during competition — endurance athletes — don't always use it. Here too the reasons are entirely related to individual differences. Some marathoners, for example, can handle sugar drinks that give other marathoners serious cramps. There is no consistent pattern of sugar use among the top endurance athletes to guide their less fleet but equally hardworking competitors who may have to eat something to stay in the contest. The one message the less fleet can get from ultraendurance athletes is to eat carbohydrates, in whatever form that is convenient and sits well in their stomachs.

New Fuel or Same Old Problem?

Lactate, or lactic acid, is a by-product of the combustion of glycogen and oxygen in hardworking muscles. For a long time, it has been thought to limit performance by accumulating in the muscles, causing pain, fatigue, and ultimately exhaustion. It has long been known that conditioned athletes clear lactate from their systems faster than the less fit. But recent research suggests that what may be happening to the lactate is that it is being burned for fuel. In fact, it may even be a fuel that some muscles, under certain stress conditions, prefer and burn more readily than glycogen. The intriguing aspect about this challenge to the existing theory of lactic acid disposal is the suggestion that lactate may be subject to nutritional manipulation. Will athletes someday be downing buffered lactic acid cocktails? There are already lactate-related substances in our diet, notably in milk. But they are digested and absorbed in simpler forms. Still, some manufacturer will no doubt soon be proclaiming the benefits of its Go-Lactic Bar, "the high-performance food no athlete can afford to be without."

It might be a bread sandwich, a banana, or even cookies or a soft drink. Or like John Erikson, who recently became the first person to swim the English Channel three times nonstop, they might sustain themselves with baby food.

The findings from the laboratory and the field suggest two training rules: First, endurance athletes must experiment with fueling up during competition to discover what their systems will handle. Second, nonendurance athletes can best protect their energy reserves with regular, high-carbohydrate eating plans.

How High Is High?

In some traditional societies, 80 percent of the calories in the average diet are from carbohydrates, and none are from refined sugar. The one such society that high-carbohydrate advocates cite most often is the Tarahumara, a tribe of Indians in northern Mexico who are among the world's greatest endurance athletes. These people engage in kickball games that last as long as forty-eight hours, with individual players covering as much as two hundred miles. What keeps them going? Their diet. It is extremely high in carbohydrates and ultralow in fats, consisting mostly of corn and beans, with additional vegetables, fruits, an occasional egg, and goat meat once or twice a year.

It isn't necessary to run with the Tarahumara to reap the benefits of their high-carbohydrate regimen, of course. But it will take time and commitment to adopt a diet so completely different from our own. And there is no evidence that we have to go to this extreme.

The question of whether it is possible to devise a calorically adequate diet that is too high in carbohydrates is a theoretical rather than a real concern. Even strict vegetarians, who eat nothing but grain products and fresh fruits and vegetables, get enough protein and fat from these foods to meet their requirements. Indeed, some get more than enough, which is why there are fat vegetarians.

The Eat-to-Win training plans are higher in complex carbohydrates than the regimens recommended by the Senate Select Committee on Nutrition and the World Health Organization. This difference guarantees abundant glycogen reserves at all times, no matter how hard we exercise or how strictly we monitor the amount we eat. As with fat intake, however, the important thing about the carbohydrate goal is to internalize it. This is one of the basic themes in chapter 12.

7

The Question of Cholesterol

If we could lower the cholesterol count of everyone in the United States below 150, we could probably wipe out heart disease.

MICHAEL DE BAKEY
Houston Medical Center

Someone who thinks he is protecting his heart by running around the track several times a week, but continues to eat a high fat diet, is just kidding himself.

RICHARD REMINGTON
University of Michigan
School of Public Health

A WOMAN IS PUSHING a shopping cart through the most spectacularly stocked supermarket you've ever seen. On either side, fruits and vegetables are stacked in perfect pyramids. She scrutinizes an array of broccoli, selects the best of the bunch, and adds it to the pile of produce in her cart. The proprietor appears. "Only the finest for you, I see," he says with an avuncular chuckle. "*You're* obviously concerned about your family's health." So saying, he thrusts a bottle of corn oil on her. "Then you'll want this." "Hmmm," she says, studying the label before she puts the bottle beside her broccoli, "and it's cholesterol-free." End of commercial.

What's wrong here, aside from the fantasy-island supermarket? Strictly speaking, it's not the commercial. It only supplies the lines. *We* read between them. What is really wrong is what is *not* being said: that discriminating, health-conscious consumers should buy cholesterol-free products because they are better for our health. Had the grocer or his customer actually stated this, the advertiser would have run afoul of the Food and Drug Administration for having made a claim that has never been proven. But so unshakable is our conviction that *cholesterol-free* means "life enhancing" that advertisers of such products have no need to make such a claim. Just give us a framework, and we'll supply the message.

The question of cholesterol exists because we have not solved our number-one health problem: heart disease. It is by far the most common cause of death in this country, and it is largely a twentieth-century phenomenon. For these reasons, health officials have often categorized the problem with a single word — *epidemic* — and researchers have been trying to identify the causes of heart disease for more than fifty years. By the exacting standards of scientific proof, there is still a lot to be learned. Nevertheless, what *is* known goes far in answering the cholesterol question, and putting it in perspective.

Studies that contrasted different countries were the first to implicate cholesterol as a contributing factor in heart disease. With few exceptions, societies with low rates of heart disease have lifestyles that are quite different from ours. They are more active, yet they eat less. Specifically, they eat a lot less fat and, more specifically, a lot less animal fat. Many of these societies also consume less sugar and salt, as well as more fiber from grains, fruits, and vegetables. But which of these factors matters most, or matters at all?

Following World War II, Dr. Ancel Keys, a noted physiologist and the developer of K rations for soldiers in the field, published a comparative study of seven countries. It documented that the societies with low-fat diets also had low levels of heart disease. Further, in all seven societies, those who died of heart disease had higher levels of cholesterol in the blood (serum cholesterol). They also had more plaque on the walls of their arteries. (Plaque is a fatty deposit, partly composed of cholesterol, that restricts the flow of blood and causes hardening of the arteries.) Keys also showed that countries with low-fat diets — diets including fat from animal foods as well as cholesterol (which is found only in animal fat) — had low levels of serum cholesterol and low levels of heart disease.

What Is Cholesterol?

Cholesterol is a fatty alcohol that the body requires for the manufacture of cell membranes, hormones, and the protective sheaths around nerve fibers; for the synthesis of vitamin D; and for the production of liver bile, which is needed to digest other forms of fat. Infants must obtain their cholesterol from dietary sources. Conveniently, mother's milk provides optimal amounts. But after the first six months, the liver makes its own cholesterol, and, theoretically, there is no longer any need for dietary cholesterol. But since it is present in almost all forms of animal fat, there is no practical way to design a cholesterol-free diet.

These basic observations have been confirmed by subsequent research, such as the Ni-Hon-San Study of three groups of Japanese. The first group, living in Japan and eating a traditional diet, consumed the least amount of animal fat and had the lowest serum cholesterol and the least heart disease. The second group, living in Honolulu and eating a mixed Japanese–American diet, consumed more animal fat and had higher serum cholesterol and more heart disease than the native Japanese. But the third group, living in San Francisco and eating an American-style diet, had the highest intake of animal fat, the highest serum cholesterol, and the most heart disease.

The link between fat and cholesterol in the diet and serum cholesterol, as well as the link between fat and cholesterol in the diet and heart disease, seemed compelling. Many health officials joined Keys in recommending a reduction in both animal fat and cholesterol, even though this diet–heart theory had not been proven. Many Americans followed the advice, as reflected by the declining sales of cholesterol-rich foods, notably the egg but also butter, cream, and high-fat meats. At the same time, the promoters of foods that had never contained a speck of cholesterol turned an unremarkable fact into an unmistakable virtue: cholesterol-free. As a result, the consumption of margarine and vegetable oils, once regarded as second-rate substitutes, began to climb. This switch from high-cholesterol foods to cholesterol-free fats has been the most dramatic change in American eating habits in the past generation. But has the change brought any benefits, or has it largely missed the point?

These may sound like fairly straightforward questions, but answering them presents tremendous difficulties. Comparative studies, by their very nature, cannot show a cause-and-effect relationship between fats and cholesterol in the diet, serum cholesterol, and heart disease. Just to acquire what researchers call a data base requires following large numbers of people over long periods.

The Framingham Study did both these things. It tracked a large, mixed population — five thousand residents of Framingham, Massachusetts — for twenty-five years, amassing an enormous amount of health-related data, including information on diet and heart disease. The study conclusively established that people with high serum cholesterol are three times as likely to have heart attacks than those with low serum cholesterol. It also identified high blood pressure (hypertension) and cigarette smoking as two other major risk factors. Also important were age (the risk of heart disease increases with age), sex (men have more heart disease than women), family medical history (heredity plays a role in the predisposition to heart disease), obesity (an indirect factor: gaining weight raises blood pressure and serum cholesterol), and personality (people with so-called Type-A, or high-stress, personalities are more prone to heart disease).

The Framingham study was not, however, designed to demonstrate whether dietary changes can reduce serum cholesterol and whether this will reduce the risk for heart disease. Again, designing such a study is a considerable challenge. No team of researchers can feed even a small group of subjects — let alone a group of five thousand — every meal of their lives for even five or ten, much less twenty-five, years. As anyone who has conducted research in human nutrition will testify, the practical alternative — relying on human recall — is an imprecise way to gather data. We have selective memories when it comes to reporting what we eat. In a study of fats and cholesterol, for example, we tend to remember the times we didn't eat eggs, meat, butter, and so forth and forget the times we did. In addition, it is difficult to study people on mixed diets and determine whether fluctuations in their serum cholesterol are due to diet or to some entirely independent factor.

As with every other aspect of nutrition and physiology, there is also the matter of individual differences. The average adult American consumes 450–600 milligrams of cholesterol per day, which is considerably less than the body produces. Normally, the body adjusts its output of cholesterol on the basis of the intake of dietary cholesterol. But how well and how rapidly this actually happens varies considerably from person to person. Some of us have serum cholesterol levels that, high or low, are unaffected by dietary cholesterol. Similarly, just as some of us have high serum cholesterol and no detectable signs of heart disease, others — like the superbly conditioned, nondrinking, nonsmoking tennis star Arthur Ashe — have massive heart attacks despite the absence of known risk factors. Add to this the fact that serum cholesterol is but *one* predictor of heart disease, and it becomes clear that designing a study to answer conclusively the diet-heart question is a practical impossibility.

Despite all these obstacles, research has yielded a consistent body of information about how dietary changes can reduce serum cholesterol. The single most important step we can take is to cut our total fat intake. Numerous studies have shown that a reduction of 50 percent can reduce serum cholesterol by 5–30 percent — in other words, the reduction of serum cholesterol is minor for some of us and major for others. What about using cholesterol-free margarines and vegetable oils? Doing so can be helpful in lowering serum cholesterol, but *only if total fat intake is reduced.* This is the point that most Americans have missed. By substituting one form of fat for another without reducing total fat intake, we do little to lower our serum cholesterol. The same is true for those who cut their use of cholesterol-rich foods without cutting their total fat intake.

In practical terms, what the studies tell us is that the one change we can make in our diet that is most likely to cause the greatest reduction in serum cholesterol is to cut substantially our consumption of saturated animal fat. This change will automatically decrease our cholesterol intake, and it will automatically increase the ratio of saturated and unsaturated fats in our diet. So, buying those "cholesterol-free" products that are "high in polyunsaturates," unless it is in the context of total fat reduction, is not part of the answer. It's part of the problem. In fact, as researchers have pointed out, the widespread use of unsaturated vegetable oils as a substi-

---

The Saturation Point

All fats are not the same. Chemically, they differ in the number of hydrogen atoms that they are "saturated" with. Most animal fats are highly saturated. Most vegetable fats are highly unsaturated; palm and coconut oils are highly saturated exceptions. The least saturated fats are the polyunsaturated vegetable oils. But when they are hydrogenated or partially hydrogenated, as in the case of margarine, they have been made somewhat more saturated with hydrogen so that they will be solid at room temperature and so that they will have a longer shelf life. Only saturated animal fats contain cholesterol.

---

tute for animal fats is a recent phenomenon whose consequences are unknown.

The question remains: Will reducing serum cholesterol reduce the risk of heart disease? Many studies have suggested that it will — at least for some people. The problem with these studies is that they look at high-risk individuals with abnormally high serum cholesterol. It's not necessarily true that what works for them will benefit those with normal serum cholesterol. Still, lowering serum cholesterol in the high-risk subjects was protective, apparently by slowing or stopping the process of plaque buildup. In one study on monkeys, a low-fat diet even reversed the process: in effect, it dissolved deposited plaque. Nathan Pritikin claims that his regimen, which drastically restricts fat, cholesterol, and salt, as well as sugar and alcohol, has the same effect on people who are actual or potential cardiac cases. So far, he has not produced any scientific data to document his contention. Assuming that he does, it could not be considered evidence that *any* diet plan can protect people from heart disease who do not have high serum cholesterol.

Information on the diet–heart question is still coming in. A recent Western Electric study analyzed the deaths of nineteen hundred middle-aged men, all of whom had been examined at least twenty years prior to their deaths. The study, one of the largest and longest of its kind, found a strong correlation between high serum cholesterol and premature death from heart disease, confirming other studies. But it also found that the men who reported that they ate less cholesterol and more polyunsaturated fats had less heart disease. The conclusion reached by these researchers was the same as Keys': "The message of these findings is that it is prudent to decrease the amount of saturated fat and cholesterol in your diet." This conclusion put them "at variance" — a nice way of saying at loggerheads — with the Food and Nutrition Board of the National Academy of Sciences, which, a year earlier, had decided that there was insufficient evidence to recommend that otherwise healthy Americans — those with no apparent heart disease and no risk factors — reduce significantly their intake of saturated fats and cholesterol.

Other studies have both clarified and complicated the diet–heart question. In 1980, a study was published that had examined nearly ten thousand Americans and Canadians who were randomly selected from various ethnic, occupational, and regional groups and thus had no particular pattern of heart disease. It focused on the blood components that carry cholesterol in the bloodstream. One kind, the high-density lipoproteins (HDLs), apparently works as a kind of intravenous SOS, scouring away the cholesterol deposits that another kind, the low-density lipoproteins (LDLs), helps to deposit. High serum cholesterol was found to go hand in hand with a high LDL level. But those people who also had a high HDL level seemed to run no extra risk of heart disease.

Are there dietary ways to increase HDL? This is what research is trying to determine. It is known that in general, women, lean people, moderate drinkers, and active people have higher HDL levels than men, overweight people, teetotalers, and inactive people. It is not known, however, whether a regimen that combines weight reduction, exercise, and moderate alcohol intake confers the protective benefits of HDLs enjoyed by people with naturally high levels.

Now consider the conviction held by many athletes that exercise is the best preventive medicine when it comes to heart disease. Exercise certainly offers a wealth of physical and psychological benefits. It can strengthen the heart (which we tend to forget is a muscle), making it more resistant to stresses that might otherwise trigger a heart attack. Yet there is also a danger of exaggerating the benefits of exercise. In the most highly regarded studies, regular, vigorous activity had a small effect in reducing the risk of death

Diet and Cancer

Although cancer kills 400,000 Americans each year, we are not in the midst of a cancer epidemic. The number of cancer deaths has been increasing since the turn of the century. The reason for this is that cancer tends to be an old-age disease, and more people are making it to old age than ever before. If age is taken into account, the cancer rate has actually declined slightly since World War II — and it would have declined more if so many women hadn't started smoking. We are not a society with a high rate of cancer. In a comparison with forty other countries, the United States ranked twentieth.

The leading cause of death from cancer in men is — and in women, soon will be — smoking. No other factor, including diet, has nearly such a clear-cut impact. But in testimony before the Senate Select Committee on Nutrition, Dr. Gio Gori, deputy director of the National Cancer Foundation, estimated that about half of the cancer cases in the United States each year appear to be related to diet. "The forms of cancer that appear to be dependent on nutrition as shown by epidemiological studies include: stomach, liver, breast, prostate, large intestine, small intestine and colon," Dr. Gori testified. He added, "We are not saying there is a direct relationship between diet and cancer. We do have strong clues that dietary factors play a predominant role in the development of these tumors."

Controversy about a diet–cancer connection is certain to go on for years. Even so, many nutritional investigators say that reducing fat, sugar, and salt while increasing complex carbohydrates in the diet offers some protection against cancer. Possibly it does. It's certainly the basis of a high-energy, Eat-to-Win regimen.

from heart disease. Exercise can raise the HDL level, but there is no evidence that the increase slows or prevents plaque production. Autopsies of young soldiers killed in Vietnam showed that the process of plaque buildup had been well under way even though the men had been in good physical condition when they were killed. No one can say which of these young men would have developed heart disease or whether the plaque in their arteries had already affected their fitness and performance. But the evidence does suggest that exercise is only one weapon in the war against heart disease.

Complicated? Then consider the findings of three reputable research teams that link low serum cholesterol with a higher incidence of cancer of the colon. These studies suggest that when it comes to cholesterol, as with other components of nutrition, too little is no better than too much.

Now for the good news: although the epidemic isn't over, death from heart disease has been declining by about 3 percent per year since the mid-1960s. No one knows for sure why this has been happening. There has been a slight decline in smoking. There have also been some changes in eating and exercising habits. There has been considerably better medical treatment for hypertension and heart disease. Researchers are currently studying these and other possible explanations. Given what is already known, it is safe to say that they will never be able to pinpoint just how — or by how much — any single factor improves the odds for avoiding heart disease. Nevertheless, even the lack of an absolute answer to the diet–heart question is no reason not to act. Research has identified a list of risk factors, and it is in the context of these factors that you can and should answer the question for yourself.

Start by assessing your risks. If you have any constitutional risks — if, for example, you are male, with a family history of heart disease — you should know what your serum cholesterol and HDL levels are. All this takes is a blood test. Even if you can't significantly reduce your serum cholesterol — and you might not be able to even by making major changes in your diet — you *can* make changes that will reduce your risk from two other major factors. Your blood pressure is simple to check, and hypertension can be controlled with medication. In fact, borderline hypertension can frequently be corrected simply by cutting salt intake and losing weight. You can also stop smoking and thereby reap a host of other health benefits as well, including a noticeable boost in your endurance.

Don't forget that heart disease has many causes. So also consider other risk factors, which are individually less critical but collectively significant. Are you overweight? Are you inactive? Do you have what some researchers call a Type-A — that is, hurried, harried, tense, high-pressure — personality and lifestyle? If so, you

Debate Goes On

At the 1981 convention of the American College of Cardiology, Dr. James A. Schoenberger, president of the American Heart Association, went to the mat with Dr. Robert E. Olson of the Food and Nutrition Board of the National Academy of Sciences. Here are excerpts from their match.

SCHOENBERGER: [The evidence is] consistent and overwhelming that ingestion of a diet high in saturated fat and cholesterol will raise the serum cholesterol of most individuals above their genetically predisposed levels and that this in turn will result in unnecessarily high levels of low-density lipoprotein, which in turn will initiate and accelerate the atherosclerotic process.

OLSON: Diet plays a role in atherogenesis, but is it so important as to warrant a public health approach based on diet? I don't think so . . . Epidemiologic associations alone, which by themselves don't prove cause and effect, are insufficient evidence for public health action. Proof of benefit should be demonstrated in some clinical trial before public health action occurs. If diet is a risk factor, one should estimate its power and not make it a monolithic approach to prevention. Is modification of fat intake the crucial element in the diet/disease association, or is it fiber, protein, carbohydrates or something else?

SCHOENBERGER: If we throw up our hands and do nothing, we'll be doing a disservice to our patients.

may have an increased potential for heart disease. To be on the safe side, get a doctor working for you. And don't be reluctant to experiment with your diet. You can drastically reduce your fat, cholesterol, and salt intake without doing yourself a bit of harm.

But what if you have none of the risk factors for heart disease? This is the case where the experts are most divided. Because having no risk factors in no way guarantees no heart disease, the American Heart Association, the Surgeon General, and the Department of Agriculture have joined with other groups in urging us to reduce our fat intake. Other equally respectable groups say there is no known benefit to merit this reduction. They also point out that all the known risk factors account for only 50 percent of the heart disease in this country. What all this adds up to is a fairly compelling argument for one of the soundest and most basic nutritional principles: moderation.

Happily, on an Eat-to-Win diet, you can have it both ways when it comes to the diet–heart question. The Eat-to-Win approach favors the use of grains and grain products, vegetables, fruits, low-fat milk and dairy products, lean meats, poultry, and fish. As a result, it is automatically significantly lower in both fat and cholesterol than the average American diet. Here's another good example of the multiple benefits of optimal nutrition: maximum energy, maximum nutrients-per-calorie, easy weight maintenance, and — just maybe — extra protection from heart disease.

8

The Neglected Nutrient

> The man who had once driven players to uncon-
> sciousness under the Texas sun hired an expert in
> tropical medicine to teach him about fluid intake,
> electrolyte balance and heat–humidity ratios.
>
> *Time* on Coach "Bear" Bryant

IF YOU HELD a contest to name the neglected nutrient, the action would be hot and heavy. Advocates of such exotic micronutrients as vitamin B-12 and zinc would passionately present their
arguments. Chapter 10 will tell you why you can safely ignore them.
You already know enough not to nominate protein, which, like fat,
sugar, and salt, is one of the most unneglected nutrients. You might
push for carbohydrates, and do so with some justification. But you
might not think of the single most important nutrient of all — water.

Most of us have never been taught to regard water as a nutrient,
let alone *the* essential one. Yet, although survival for weeks is possible without any other nutrient, only a few days without water can
be fatal.

The body is 67 percent water, and all the complex chemical cou-
plings, bondings, exchanges, and transfers of energy that constitute
the metabolic process occur in the sustaining medium of water. We
require it to digest food, to carry nutrients to our cells, and to flush
wastes from our bodies. Finally, we need water to regulate our
internal temperatures.

How vital is water to athletes? More contests are lost through
dehydration — water loss — than for any other nutritional reason.
If we are undernourished or even just under the weather, we can
still compete. But if we are underhydrated, we can easily find our-

91

selves out of the game altogether. Even a slight water loss is enough to put a big dent in performance. When it amounts to 1–2 percent of body weight, pulse and temperature go up. Two percent represents the fluid reserves that are most readily available to the body, and some researchers think that conditioned athletes may actually perform a bit more efficiently at this slight degree of dehydration. Beyond this level, however, all experts agree that dehydration is increasingly detrimental. At a loss of 5 percent — the amount of water that can be easily lost in a tennis match on a hot, humid day — the ability to perform hard work drops 20–30 percent. If we are in condition and accustomed to the heat, the water loss will not noticeably affect our motor-muscle functions. But a loss of 8 percent of body weight probably will, and may also lead to cramps, exhaustion, nausea, and dizziness, the classic symptoms of heat illness.

Dehydration hinders performance by impairing the body's ability to keep cool. To function at its best, the body must regulate its temperature within fairly narrow limits. For most of us most of the time, the range is 98.6 degrees plus or minus 1 degree. If we exceed the limit by only a few degrees, our muscles work less efficiently. At 105–106 degrees or so, they stop altogether, because we lose consciousness. And when our internal temperature rises much above 108 degrees our brains literally start to cook.

Fortunately, we are equipped with sensitive cooling systems that function well under a wide variety of conditions. These systems are routinely overextended by hardworking athletes, though. For this reason, it's essential to understand how the cooling system operates and how we can keep it operating even in the worst of circumstances.

The body is a heat machine. In fact, 75 percent of all the energy we burn winds up as heat. Even when we are asleep, our internal organs generate heat. Any time we are active, our working muscles generate a great deal more. The bloodstream, which brings oxygen to the muscles so that fuel can be converted to energy, also transports heat from the muscles. The heated blood continues to circulate through the body. When it reaches the hypothalamus in the brain, a chain of events is set off. The hypothalamus, the body's thermostat, measures the heat buildup. In short order, it responds by instructing the blood vessels just under the skin to dilate a certain amount. It also tells the heart to pump harder to bring more blood to the skin surface. (As a result, hardworking athletes look flushed.) Finally, it signals some or all of the three million sweat glands to produce sweat. As sweat evaporates from the outer surface of the skin, the blood is cooled and then cycled back to the core of the body.

Sweating is the working body's most efficient form of cooling. But how hard and how well we will sweat on a given occasion depends on a number of factors: our fitness, the weather, our workload, our energy reserves, and our fluid reserves.

Fitness. When we are in good shape, so are our cooling systems. When we are well-conditioned, we store more fluids and our cardiovascular systems are more efficient. Sweating begins sooner and is more efficient. As a result, our internal temperature is lower, and we are able to tolerate better the effects of dehydration. All these processes are even more efficient when we are fully weather conditioned. We'll sweat more efficiently on a typically hot August day than on an unseasonal but equally hot April or October day, just because we are acclimatized. It takes time to acclimatize — about two weeks of gradually increasing the intensity of training, not a day or two. Age is also a factor in sweating, for heat tolerance, cardiovascular fitness, and all other physical processes decline with age. Body fat matters too, because it acts as insulation.

Weather. Heat and humidity are the enemies of active athletes. The higher the external temperature, the greater the internal heat buildup and the harder it is to dispose of the excess heat. The higher the humidity, the more slowly sweat evaporates. It evaporates even more slowly when there is no wind. As the heat and humidity climb, the body's cooling system must compensate by diverting more blood to the skin (leaving less for the muscles) and instructing the heart and sweat glands to work harder. At this point, sweat starts to pour out, and it's as far from a "good, healthy sweat" as it can be. First, the body is losing fluids at a very rapid rate. Second, beads of sweat inhibit rather than enhance cooling. They either roll off the skin altogether or evaporate far more slowly than a film of sweat of the same volume but with a much greater surface area.

Workload. The harder and longer we exercise, the greater our internal heatload and the more we sweat to dispose of it. Once again, more blood is diverted to the skin — as much as 25 percent of our total volume in the most demanding situations. Even when the percentage is less, our performance is limited by the amount of oxygenated blood that reaches our muscles.

Energy Reserves. Because sweating is automatic, it's easy not to appreciate how it can sap strength and stamina. When we're hot, our hearts work harder, and our other muscles work less efficiently. Our three million sweat glands also need energy to operate. As the weather and workload increase the demands on our cooling systems, they restrict the amount of energy that is available for the task at hand.

Fluid Reserves. Like a car without a radiator cap, we always lose fluid when we sweat. As already pointed out, dehydration has an increasingly detrimental impact on health and performance. The primary problem is that some of the fluid we lose is from the bloodstream itself. Thus, blood volume decreases, and blood becomes thicker and harder to pump. Less oxygen flows to the brain and muscles, and less heat is carried to the surface of the skin. As a result, the internal body temperature rises still more, and the cooling system is forced to work even harder with even less fluid. While this is happening internally, we experience one or more of the classic symptoms of heat exhaustion: headache, weakness, cramps, dizziness, blurred vision. Finally, the body can no longer supply the brain, the muscles, and the skin with enough blood. It makes a lifesaving decision, and we faint from heat exhaustion. This form of heat illness is serious, but it also protects us from the far more serious risks of heatstroke.

It is at this point that determined, conditioned athletes can get themselves in trouble, because they can push past the point at which others would faint. In so doing, they push their luck. They are not far from forcing their bodies to make a last desperate attempt to maintain circulation — by shutting down the sweat glands to prevent further fluid loss. When this happens, the internal body temperature quickly climbs beyond the danger point. This profound disruption of the heat-regulating system is called heatstroke. It is one of the most common causes of death among athletes — *yet it is entirely preventable.*

We can avoid the damage of dehydration and the danger of heat illness simply by maintaining our fluid levels. Yet there are enough myths and misunderstandings about fluid intake, absorption, and

---

Heat Illness: Symptoms and Treatment

Heat exhaustion

Symptoms: pale, clammy skin; heavy sweating; weakness, possibly muscle cramps; headache. *Treatment:* rest and plenty of liquids, particularly juices to replace electrolytes.

Heatstroke

Symptoms: very high temperature; hot, dry skin; rapid pulse; possibly convulsions and loss of consciousness. *Treatment:* quickly lowering the victim's body temperature by wetting or immersion in water or any liquid, or with fan or air conditioner; fluids if conscious; medical assistance as quickly as possible.

---

retention that this simple advice can seem complex. Here are some easy-to-follow guidelines.

Before

1. *Anticipate your fluid needs.* A little experience and a look at the weather should give you some idea of how much you're going to sweat. A more nearly precise prediction can be made by checking the temperature–humidity index, commonly called the THI. Almost always included in weather forecasts, it provides a "comfort" measurement. When the THI is over 75, almost everyone is uncomfortable. If you exercise, you will sweat heavily. The chart on page 96 is a guide to the degree of caution you should observe.

Not surprisingly, an 80-degree day with 60 percent humidity is in the caution zone. So is a 60-degree day with 80 percent humidity. The so-called caution zone is actually quite narrow, and this in itself presents dangers. Only mad dogs and marathoners go out in an oppressively hot midday sun. The rest of us wait until it doesn't feel so hot. Just as we can get our worst sunburns on hazy days when we forget how much ultraviolet radiation is actually getting through, we can become severely dehydrated on days when the temperature and humidity fall just on the safe side of the caution zone. These are the days when we can easily fail to take precautions.

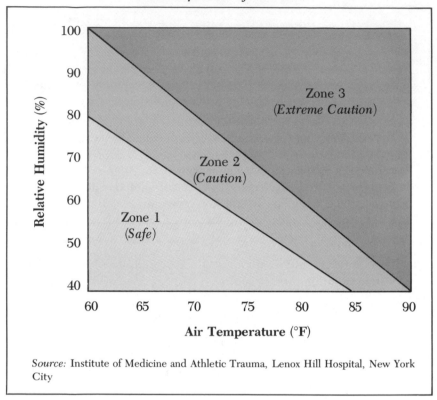

Source: Institute of Medicine and Athletic Trauma, Lenox Hill Hospital, New York City

2. *"Force" liquids.* You've considered the temperature and humidity, the task at hand, and such personal factors as your fitness. The signs all point to heavy sweating. Now what? Now you can plan ahead to compete in a state of optimal hydration.

A lot of athletes find it hard to believe that drinking as much as a half-gallon of water a half-hour before a contest will improve performance when heavy sweating is anticipated. But it will. In fact, drinking almost that much just five or ten minutes before competition will have no negative effects beyond the discomfort of a distended stomach. Though not a recommended training practice, it's a lot better than the effects of drinking too little. There's a common conviction that drinking a lot of water before exercise will cause cramps or excessive sweating. It will do neither. A very few athletes may get headaches from drinking huge amounts of water. This effect of "water intoxication" is caused by a temporary mineral imbalance inside and outside the cells. The solution is to drink less water at any one time or to drink a mineral-rich fruit juice. This rare exception aside, it is next to impossible to waterlog a healthy athlete, whose kidneys will quickly clear away any excess. Naturally, you don't want to exercise or compete with a full bladder, but you do want to be as fully hydrated as possible. Here's how.

You know you're going to be sweating heavily, so you've sensibly been "forcing" fluids well in advance. About ten minutes before exertion, drink as much as two glasses of water on an empty bladder. Ten minutes allows enough time for the fluid to get out of your stomach but not through your kidneys. Once you start exercising, your kidneys will slow or shut down, producing little or no urine; so you will be starting with a maximum fluid reserve. This is always the goal, and it takes the same kind of practice you devote to other aspects of training. If experience shows that you can exceed the rule of thumb of two glasses in ten minutes, do so. By forcing fluids in hot and humid weather, you will get the biggest possible head start.

3. *Eat carbohydrates.* Although it is always advisable to exercise on an empty stomach, your day-to-day diet can increase not only your energy reserves but your fluid reserves as well. A high-carbohydrate diet helps you store glycogen in your liver and muscles. The storage process also binds water — as much as two to three extra quarts — which can then be released during exercise. This benefit does not require strict carbohydrate loading. A regular high-carbohydrate regimen — the kind that provides a host of other advantages — also increases your water reserves.

4. *Plan ahead for water availability.* Even the rankest of amateurs can have professional attitudes about sports. When it comes to water, this means making sure that you or the organizer of the event has provided ample water supplies. Failure to do so is a mark of ignorance, a lack of professionalism, and a threat to health and optimal performance. There will always be someone around who will tell you that exercising without water is better for you or that it's a test of character. Such advice is dead wrong, and sometimes even deadly.

During

1. *Drink before you feel thirsty.* Although the hypothalamus is a reliable thermostat, it is not dependable as a thirst regulator. Like hunger, thirst is a signal that is slow to register and easy to ignore. You can have a water deficit as high as 4 percent of your body weight yet not feel thirsty. Caught up in the excitement of the game, you may lose even more water than this without noticing how thirsty you are and how dehydrated you've become. (The process can also work in reverse: pregame jitters can give you cotton mouth when in fact your body is adequately hydrated.) A reliable signal that it is time to drink is sweating itself. Noticeable sweating is a sign that you need to replace fluid.

2. *Drink more than your thirst requires.* Not only is the sensation of thirst slow to register; it can also shut off prematurely. So quenching your thirst does not mean you are adequately rehydrated. The thirst signal, in fact, shuts off when you've replaced only about half the fluid you've lost. For this reason alone, always drink more than you think you need.

How much more? This is yet another instance when standards are of little use to athletes. Usually, we need two and a half to three quarts of water per day to be properly hydrated. Much of this liquid comes from food: most vegetables are 90 percent water; a baked potato is 75 percent water; plain bread is 33 percent water. In addition, nutritionists advise us to drink six to eight glasses of fluid a day. They add that active athletes need a great deal more — usually more than they can conveniently replace when they're working and sweating hard. The issue, then, is not how much you need but how much you can replace.

In most competitive situations, you should be able to drink as much as two glasses of water every ten to fifteen minutes without feeling bloated. That's about sixteen ounces — or, to be more realistic, sixteen gulps (at one gulp per ounce) or forty-eight sips (at three sips per ounce) at the water fountain. Endurance athletes, however, have a harder time replacing lost body fluid. The more rigorous and continuous the exercise, the more slowly fluid moves out of the digestive system and into the body. The reason for this is that the body is directing as much blood as possible to the brain and muscles, as well as to the skin for cooling, and almost none to the digestive system. As a result, marathoners and other high-intensity endurance athletes cannot absorb more than about a quart of water per hour.

Considering all these variables — the weather, the nature of your sport, the way you play, and so forth — it's impossible to predict how much fluid you'll have to replace at any one time. On the other hand, it's a safe bet to say that you'll need more than you think. So drink whenever you can.

3. *Drink plain water.* Plain water is always the best fluid to drink during exercise. The key issue here is how fast the fluid will get out of the stomach, into the bloodstream, and to the tissues. Faster is better, and several factors influence the rate of gastric emptying. One, as just noted, is how hard and continuously you're exercising. Another is volume. Large amounts of fluid empty faster than small amounts. A third is temperature. Cold drinks empty fastest, and they also reduce the temperature of the stomach lining (this produces a welcome cooling effect) and thereby increase its absorbency. (And, contrary to popular belief, ice-cold water or even ice cubes do not cause cramps.) Finally, the caloric value of the drink has a profound effect on gastric emptying.

Many athletes realize that after two hours or more of hard, steady exercise, they deplete their glycogen reserves; so they try to offset this loss with sweetened drinks. They think they are meeting two needs at once — energy and water — but they are misguided on both counts. Sugar in any form — glucose, fructose, or sucrose — *slows* gastric emptying, and it doesn't take much to do so.

Taking the pause that refreshes during hard, steady exercise can cause you to lose your competitive edge. In fifteen minutes, your stomach will absorb only 5 percent of a can of cola, compared with 60–70 percent of the same amount of water. Studies have shown that a 10 percent glucose solution slows the rate of gastric emptying by 50 percent. When the glucose content is 15 percent, the rate at which the stomach empties is only 20 percent of what it is for plain water. Drinks that are no more than 2.5 percent sugar can be absorbed almost as fast as water. This is why some endurance athletes drink fruit juice or "defizzed" cola diluted with at least twice as much water. (Why defizzed? Carbonation slows gastric emptying and causes a "gassy" feeling. Why cola? For the caffeine. See chapter 11.) Such drinks provide them fewer than 5 calories per ounce, or about 160 calories per hour at a strong and steady pace.

In any endurance event, digestion is practically at a standstill. So the amount of caloric energy that can be absorbed is not very significant. High-calorie drinks increase the risk of stomach cramps. And, in an effort to dilute the calories, even though they are in liquid form, the stomach draws fluid from the rest of the body. This is clearly counterproductive — and another reason why plain water is the wisest choice during endurance exercise.

The question of calories during discontinuous, stop-and-go sports is a lot less critical. Digestion (as well as the kidneys) switches to "hold" only when output is high. Thus, the question here is, Do you need extra calories? Unless you've skipped a meal, you have more than adequate energy reserves for almost every contingency. So you probably don't need extra calories.

Even in less intense sports, there are fluids that you should avoid. If you're thinking about a beer, save the thought until after the game. Among its numerous performance drawbacks, alcohol significantly reduces heat tolerance. In addition, like the caffeine in cola, coffee, and tea, alcohol is a diuretic, which promotes dehydration by increasing urination.

4. *Minimize sweating.* Too many athletes equate working up a good sweat with a good workout. Because they think of sweating as a necessary component of conditioning, they promote the process. They can be found in almost any gym, encased in sweat suits and dripping with perspiration. They may explain that they're conditioning. And they are — if they're planning to play in the tropics. They may say they're "spot" reducing, even though the body cannot be prodded or programmed into losing fat selectively. They may point out that they're losing weight. And they are — water weight via dehydration. This may be just what they want if they're trying to make a certain weight category fast. The most important thing they all are losing is the chance to perform at their best.

Although it is an essential and automatic process, sweating nevertheless consumes a considerable amount of energy. To encourage the process beyond what is necessary is to steal your own energy — energy that you could use to improve your strength, stamina, and skill.

Football coaches, from Bear Bryant on down, have learned this lesson the hard way. It was once common to see players fully suited up and working out under a broiling summer sun. As a result, thousands of young athletes suffered from heat exhaustion and heatstroke every year. In fact, between 1965 and 1975, heat illness was second only to spinal injuries as the most common cause of death in high-school athletics. Now, coaches worth their salt know that replacing fluid is essential to a team's health and performance. The really smart ones have learned the competitive advantages of conserving fluid as well.

Simple things, such as staying out of the sun whenever possible — running beneath trees, practicing early or late in the day, and so forth — can conserve a lot of water. So can wearing as little clothing as your modesty and sport allows. As long as the sun isn't beating down on you, bare skin is the best conductor of heat. Make sure that what you do wear is light, porous, and loose so that air can circulate over your skin and so that heat isn't trapped between your skin and clothing. Light colors reflect the sun better than dark colors, and white is best of all.

Another way to conserve water is to warm up without working up a sweat. Pacing is important too. A fast start on a hot day generates a surge of inner heat. Starting off slowly and pacing yourself in the heat guarantees that you'll sweat more efficiently in the long run. Finally, don't miss a chance to get wet. Water also cools from the outside and it promotes the cooling process of evaporation.

After

1. *Replace fluids.* On hot or humid days, you lose a lot more water than you realize. You can prove or disprove this with a simple experiment: weigh yourself before and after you exercise. The difference is due almost entirely to dehydration. (Exercise burns calories, but you have to go all out to lose more than a quarter-pound an hour.) This is the amount of fluid you need to replace, and you should train yourself to make such replacement an integral part of your training regimen.

2. *Replace electrolytes.* Sweat is more than water. It also contains minute amounts of minerals, notably sodium, potassium,

magnesium, calcium, and phosphorus. In water, these electrolytes conduct the tiny electrical currents that carry information along the nerves and signal the muscles to contract. Anything that affects the muscles is of obvious interest to athletes. And maintaining the proper electrolyte balance is essential to health and performance.

How is electrolyte balance best restored? The answer is clear, according to a recent ad for Gatorade. It showed a parched runner under a red-hot sun. The headline stated, "By the time your mouth gets thirsty, your body could be two quarts low." The ad asserted that Gatorade is superior to soft drinks, juices, and water, and the thrust of the ad clearly suggested that Gatorade is the ideal running companion.

Actually, Gatorade is only the first and best-known of a number of commercial electrolyte-replacement drinks. All of them contain essentially the same ingredients, though the proportions differ (and much is made of this fact in their ads). All contain sugar, not so much for "quick energy" (the original Gatorade contained artificial sweeteners) as for flavor (without sugar, they would taste like bilge water). Sugar is their first and biggest drawback, especially for that parched runner shown in the ad. The amount of sugar in these drinks is more than enough to produce a drastic slowing of gastric emptying, as well as to induce stomach cramps. Their salt content would put that same runner at a double disadvantage, since it too slows gastric emptying.

Salt (sodium chloride) is the main source of sodium in the American diet. It is also the substance that most people associate with sweating, simply because sweat tastes salty. After periods of heavy sweating, a pinch of salt per quart of water is recommended by some nutritionists. Others say it is simpler to use a little more table salt at mealtime. The best thing to do is simply forget about it. The sodium from salt is the most dangerously overabundant mineral in your diet, and you'd have a hard time designing a regimen that has no added salt — just ask anyone whose doctor has prescribed one. Even if you could, you'd probably get enough sodium from the raw and lightly processed foods you would be eating. And if you didn't, your body would inform you in a simple, straightforward way: you would crave salt.

Too much salt in the system is a bigger threat than too little, especially when the salt comes from salt tablets. In such concentrated form, salt is corrosive in the stomach and forces large amounts of fluid to be drawn there from the body. Salt tablets also increase the risk of heatstroke, heart attack, kidney failure, and blood clots. In other words, *never take salt tablets.*

Overconcern with salt has overshadowed the most important electrolyte that athletes lose during exercise: potassium. When heat builds up in the body during exercise, the muscles release potassium, which improves circulation by causing the veins to dilate. Too much potassium in the blood, however, can interfere with the heart's contractions. For this reason, potassium is eliminated in sweat and urine. Potassium depletion impairs the muscles' ability to use glycogen. This impairment, in turn, impairs performance. But your muscles will contain ample potassium reserves to see them through even the longest race if you regularly replace potassium after you exercise. The best sources are fruits and vegetables, which have the added nutritional advantage of containing other minerals, fiber, and complex carbohydrates. Commercial electrolyte drinks also contain potassium. Like salt tablets, potassium supplements are a terrible idea and can raise the level of potassium in the blood to a level that can cause heart failure. As with most components of nutrition, overdosing is as harmful as depletion. Remember that the issue is to restore your electrolyte *balance.*

Calcium, magnesium, and phosphorus are abundant even in the less-than-ideal average American diet. They are often in our drinking water as well. They need be of no concern. Although they aren't necessary in electrolyte drinks, they probably don't do any harm. In supplemental form, however, they can act as laxatives.

To the same degree that electrolytes were once ignored, they are now heavily promoted as precious minerals. This they are. Yet, with the possible exception of potassium, they are also abundant in everyone's diet. It's true that heavy and repeated bouts of sweating *can* deplete electrolyte reserves, specifically and most probably the potassium reserve. It's also true that conditioned, acclimatized athletes not only sweat more efficiently but also conserve electrolytes better than others. The symptoms of sodium and potassium depletions are the same: muscle weakness and fatigue. To cure them, let your taste buds dictate your need for salt, and depend on fruits, fruit juices, and vegetables for potassium. Drink commercial electrolyte drinks if you want, but remember that they are counter-productive during continuous exercise, cost money, and are (pun intended) second-rate solutions to the problem of electrolyte replacement. Nature has provided us with ideal sources, and they are especially abundant and affordable during the season when we most need them.

9

The Necessary
Non–nutrient

There are only two things I demand of a diet: one,
that it allow me to have a good bowel movement
before I race and, two, that it cause no distress
while I'm running.

GEORGE SHEEHAN
Medical Editor, *Runner's World*

UNDERSTANDABLY, SCIENTISTS HAVE tended to focus on the
roles that essential nutrients play in health and performance. The
idea that something else might be needed — something without
nutritional value yet invaluable to health — is relatively new. It is
now known that there is at least one such substance: fiber. Although it is not a nutrient, it is essential in the diet. Perhaps its
importance was overlooked for so long because it had been a given
in the average diet — until relatively recently.

Fiber — what our grandparents called roughage — is the struc-
tural part of whole grains, vegetables, fruits, nuts, and seeds, the
part that cannot be digested. Some fiber is found in all plant foods,
but there is practically none in meat, fish, poultry, milk and dairy
products, and highly processed foods of all kinds.

A lot of the current enthusiasm for fiber stems from studies of
African tribes. Researchers have discovered that tribal Africans —
those still living much as their ancestors did centuries ago — are
rarely bothered by heart disease, hernias, appendicitis, diverticulitis, polyps, or cancer of the colon. All these diseases are common
in more advanced societies, and they also occur in Africans who

105

have left their tribes and moved to modern cities. These differing disease patterns can be explained in part by the fact that tribal Africans lead a more active life, and therefore derive the cardiovascular benefits of regular, rigorous exercise. But a comparison of the two diets, tribal and urban, has revealed another major difference: the tribal diet is as much as 600 percent higher in fiber.

These findings have caused many nutritionists to reconsider the ramifications of what they had known for years — namely, that fiber is a missing ingredient in the average American diet. Over the past half-century, our eating habits have changed radically, and they have changed in favor of foodstuffs without fiber and ones from which the fiber has been removed. This is especially true of the food that was once considered the staff of life — bread.

The milling of grain into flour is older than recorded history, and probably as old as settled civilization itself. Like any form of processing, it removes nutrients. Whole-grain flour is still highly nutritious, however, although not quite as nutritious as whole grains themselves. Unlike unmilled grains, flour can be stored for long periods without spoiling. This in itself makes milling a more than acceptable trade-off from a nutritional point of view.

Traditionally, milling has been time-consuming. Initially, simple economics dictated the *minimum* processing possible to remove the fat-containing part of the wheat germ, the edible part of the grain. Minimal processing resulted in a coarse, dark flour. With extra milling, a finer-grained white flour could be produced. But it was expensive, and white bread was, therefore, a luxury associated with the privileged classes. Then, about a century ago, milling technology improved to the extent that white flour became almost as cheap as whole-grain flour. Not surprisingly, consumers flocked to the highly refined flour, which had for so long been associated with high refinement. In upwardly mobile America, white bread soon became the standard.

Popularity and availability soon stripped white bread of its snob appeal. Consumers failed to appreciate at the time that the extra refining that was necessary to produce white flour also stripped it of most of its vitamins and all of its fiber. When nutritionists pointed this out to millers and bakers, they responded by adding vitamins to their overprocessed product. The result was what is now called enriched white bread. The process of enriching commercially baked bread and other grain products largely restored these foodstuffs to their proper nutritional niche. What was not restored, of course, was the fiber that had been lost in processing. This might not have been a problem had Americans not also developed a preference for highly processed fruits and vegetables around the same time. Deficient in nutrients and fiber, these too contributed to the fiber deficit in the American diet.

Belated recognition of the deficit, coupled with an appreciation of the apparent benefits of a high-fiber "tribal" diet, has led to a rediscovery of fiber, the necessary non-nutrient. The event has, in recent years, assumed the aspects of a nutritional "second coming" in some quarters: enthusiasts hail fiber as everything from a "nutritional superstar" to "the key to a long, healthy life" to "the most exciting medical story of the 1970s." It has also led to some bizarre developments in the marketplace, the oddest of which is a bread with "twice the fiber" of ordinary bread. What the manufacturer does not tell us, however, is that the added fiber is wood pulp, not grain husks. We would derive the same benefits from eating sawdust. To be able to evaluate the hype and hoopla, it's necessary to know the facts about fiber — what it does as well as what it does not do in the body.

In the digestive system, fiber is like a sponge, absorbing many times its weight of water. The result is a larger, softer, heavier stool, one that moves more rapidly through the digestive system. (If your grandmother was one who called fiber roughage, she may also have referred to fiber as nature's broom. The expression does not accurately describe fiber's action in the intestines, but it does describe its effect.) The absorptive properties of fiber have a number of known and theoretical health benefits. One of the obvious benefits is that fiber promotes regularity. And because it increases stool size and softness, it can prevent the formation of hemorrhoids. When hemorrhoids already exist, as a direct result of straining hard to expel, fiber minimizes the distress associated with such herniated tissue.

Fiber also alleviates the discomfort that results from diverticulitis, a common ailment in older Americans. Diverticulitis is an inflammation of the intestines caused when small pouches in the intestines trap and hold food, thereby becoming infected. Ironically, in the past the treatment for diverticulitis was a low-fiber diet, which was prescribed on the theory that it was fiber that was being trapped. Modern medicine has found exactly the opposite: fiber keeps the easily infected pockets clean.

A high-fiber diet may also be effective in the treatment of some forms of diabetes. Because high-fiber, high-carbohydrate foods are converted more gradually into blood sugar than other foods are, they are recommended for diabetics, who have trouble regulating their blood sugar levels. The sugar from an apple, for example, enters the system more gradually than the sugar from an equivalent amount of apple juice. (The high-fiber apple also satisfies hunger better than apple juice.) The moderating effect of a high-fiber diet on blood sugar is important not only to diabetics but to athletes as well. (As pointed out in chapter 6, maintaining a steady blood sugar level is an important aspect of efficient energy production.)

Fiber's role in preventing colon and rectal cancer, the third most common cause of cancer-related deaths, has not been scientifically demonstrated, although the theory is both concise and plausible. By moving food quickly through the digestive tract, the theory suggests, fiber reduces the transit time of everything we eat, including potential toxins and carcinogens. When these toxins linger in our systems too long on too many occasions over too many years, scientists speculate, the chance that they will eventually cause cancer increases. If true, this is certainly one more reason to eat a high-fiber diet.

Does fiber have anything to offer athletes in particular? If you and George Sheehan are on the same wavelength — if you have ever been bothered by irregularity or constipation — the answer is yes. Fiber practically guarantees regularity. A high-fiber, low-fat meal also leaves the stomach quickly. This is important because it is best to compete on an empty stomach yet get food, and thus its energy, into the system as close to the time of competition as possible.

Fiber can also help if you are watching your weight or trying to lose weight. All high-fiber foods are, bite for bite, more filling and less caloric than others. Because fiber expands in the stomach, you feel fuller on fewer calories. Even more to the point for the dieting *athlete*, high-fiber foods are rich in the complex carbohydrates required to maintain steady energy production.

If fiber belongs in an optimal diet, how much do you need? By now, you should be skeptical of specific, everyday nutritional recommendations. Some nutritionists say about 5 grams of fiber per day is adequate. But you don't have to be a mathematician to eat the right amount of fiber. You can just follow these simple guidelines.

1. *Eat a variety of fiber foods.* Eating a high-variety diet is the most effective way to get the necessary non-nutrient, as well as nutrients. When most people think of fiber, they think of bran. But bran contains only one of five different kinds of dietary fiber, each of which has different properties and effects. The kind of fiber that is in a food can also differ, depending on whether it's eaten raw or cooked, and on how it's cooked. There aren't even accepted standards for fiber content. The amount of crude fiber in a food, which is listed on some cereal boxes, is considered a useless measurement by most nutritionists, because the measuring process itself destroys certain forms of fiber. Dietary fiber is the total of all forms. Here too, however, the measuring process is imperfect, and different testers get different results. Finally, some of the evidence suggests that the *kinds* of fiber we get may be more important than the total *amount.* So, while the experts continue their research, don't drive yourself bananas (which contain one form of fiber) trying to keep track of the amount and kinds of fiber you eat. Simply follow the high-variety principle, which is the cornerstone of optimal nutrition. Eat a variety of whole-grain foods and fresh fruit and vegetables every day.

2. *Assess your regularity.* There are plenty of cultures that consider what they *don't* digest as meaningful a measure of well-being as what they *do* digest. Contrarily, our society, as reflected by Madison Avenue, is exceedingly concerned with constipation and irregularity. Active athletes are less likely to be bothered by these ailments because their digestion is more efficient. But if you have to use a laxative or enema, you would benefit from more fiber in your diet.

3. *Don't take fiber pills, supplements, and laxatives.* If you want to add fiber to your diet, you can, of course, buy unprocessed bran to sprinkle on or stir into food, pop fiber pills, or turn to laxatives. But if your eating patterns are reasonably on target, none of these is necessary. Chemical laxatives have an added drawback: they

can create a laxative dependency by causing the digestive system to lose efficiency and become dependent on artificial stimulation. Nonchemical laxatives (the ones that boast how naturally gentle they are) are made of vegetable fiber that has been extracted, packaged, promoted, and sold at inflated prices. Eating the vegetables in the first place would give you the same fiber plus a wide variety of important nutrients.

The issue of laxatives is especially relevant to older athletes. As we age, our salivary glands become less efficient, and swallowing what we eat becomes more difficult. To compensate, many older people turn to soft, highly processed foods, which are higher in calories, lower in nutrients, and devoid of fiber. They must then deal with the constipation that such a diet promotes, and they often do so with laxatives. What they really require is fewer calories (the need for which gradually declines with age), more nutrients (the need for which remains constant), and more fiber. They could satisfy all these needs by switching to an all-bran cereal, fresh, ripe fruits, and steamed vegetables, which are high in fiber, soft, and easy to swallow.

4. *Don't eat too much fiber.* An excess of fiber is not the solution to a deficit. Wheat, for example, contains phytates, substances that can bind with such minerals as calcium, iron, and zinc and prevent their absorption. If you were to eat enough wheat to develop a deficiency of any of these minerals, however, you'd probably find that so much fiber made you bloated and "gassy." A certain amount of flatulence is normal when beginning a higher-fiber regimen. It disappears quickly, as soon as the intestinal flora have adjusted to the change in diet. Like high variety, moderation is a nutritional rule that applies to the non-nutrient.

A fiber fad has been growing in this country since the early 1970s. When all the hype has died down, will fiber be an everyday component of everyone's diet? Let's hope so. But what fiber is not and will never be is a nutritional cure-all. There is no nutritional cure-all, and there never will be. The best evidence, though not conclusive, suggests that a moderate amount of dietary fiber from a variety of foods is a sensible form of health insurance. The best way to get as much of the necessary non-nutrient you need is to follow the eating patterns recommended in this book.

10

A to Zinc: The Micronutrients

> No normal person who is eating properly has to take any supplementary vitamins or minerals. In fact, the American food supply is so abundant and diversified, and so many staple foods have been fortified with supplemental vitamins and minerals, that it is actually difficult to avoid getting enough.
>
> RALPH LEE SMITH
> *The Health Hucksters*

> American athletes have the most expensive urine in the world.
>
> VARIOUS SOURCES

ARCHAEOLOGISTS OF THE FUTURE, sifting through the popular literature of late-twentieth-century American civilization, may well conclude that our main nutritional problem was the lack of vitamins and minerals in our daily diet. Upon closer inspection, however, they would discover how the micronutrients, surrounded by myths and misunderstandings, transformed otherwise normal people into nutritional neurotics.

Science now knows of some forty vitamins and minerals that play subtle and complex roles in practically every physical process. In 1913 a vitamin was isolated for the first time. (This is the one dubbed A.) Until that time, scientists had only speculated that there were substances in the diet that might prevent or cure certain diseases. By the 1930s, researchers had succeeded in duplicating the chemical structure of vitamins in the laboratory. This event was to have tremendous practical significance.

The country was in the grip of the Great Depression, and certain vitamin deficiencies were a legitimate health problem. Inexpensive white bread lost most of its B vitamins in processing. In areas where green, leafy vegetables were not readily available or easily affordable, there were also deficiencies of vitamin A. And many children, forced to work, weren't able to get vitamin D in the simplest way: from the action of the sun on the skin.

The medical community proposed an elegant solution: add synthetic vitamins to basic foods — A and D to milk and the B complex to grain products. These simple steps virtually eliminated vitamin-deficiency diseases in this country. Not eliminated, however, was the growing micronutrient mythology, a grab bag of misconceptions promoted by a new breed of snake-oil salesmen, the health hucksters.

The original health-food enthusiasts were concerned about the effects of poor eating patterns and overprocessing on the national health. In the hands of the hucksters, this concern soon escalated into an industry. The growing ranks of nutrition-conscious Americans were soon being informed that their food supply was suspect and responsible for such nebulous but nagging problems as tired blood. Fortunately, they were told, there was a vitamin or mineral, or an all-natural, organic product that could cure everything that ailed them.

Charlatans, especially when cloaked in scientific-sounding jargon, are able to exploit eager but uninformed consumers by playing to their ignorance and to their understandable desire for a shortcut to better health. They have profited from the constitutional right to spout nonsense, but they have prospered also because of the lack of knowledge about how micronutrients do what they do. Still, there is a lot that science does know — more than enough, in fact, to help us assess when and why the micronutrients might and might not merit our concern.

Much of the current popular thinking about vitamins and minerals can be summarized in three sentences: (1) They promote health and prevent disease. (2) We probably don't get enough of them because of the way our food is grown, because of our eating habits, and because our lives are stressful. (3) Supplements are a safe way to ensure that we get enough of them. If this seems a logical progression, it should. It has been the message from the makers of supplements, enriched foods, and "health" foods for more than half a century. If the billions of dollars we spend on these items every year is any indication, the suppliers have been phenomenally successful. But, under closer scrutiny, does the logic of these statements hold up?

Micronutrients, Health, and Disease

Vitamins are organic molecules and minerals inorganic molecules that the body cannot manufacture but requires in extremely small amounts. Their primary functions are to regulate the metabolic processes governing growth, maintenance, and repair. The specific roles of each vitamin and mineral are only partially understood. It *is* known, however, that micronutrients are team players — that is, they work in combination in complicated ways with other nutrients. This is only one reason why overconcern about a single micronutrient is frequently misleading.

As with the other nutrients, our bodies can comfortably adapt to a wide range of available micronutrients. If the supply is on the low side, we absorb, store, and use micronutrients more efficiently. If the supply is overabundant, we store them in varying amounts and excrete the rest. Even when a vitamin or mineral is nearly or completely absent — a condition that can occur only in a controlled laboratory setting — it takes months to years for a deficiency to manifest itself. The body's ability to store micronutrients is an important reason why a day-to-day concern with vitamin and mineral intake is unwarranted as long as the overall, long-range eating patterns are adequate.

Still, most of us have the same eating patterns from day to day. For this reason, an average daily need for micronutrients has been established by the World Health Organization and similar groups. In the United States, the RDAs suggested by the National Research Council are widely accepted. The RDA of a given nutrient is almost certainly a good deal more than you need, since it includes a generous safety margin to guarantee that it is sufficient to meet the needs of practically everyone in practically every condi-

Recommended Daily Dietary Allowances
(Revised 1980)

	Age (years)	Weight (lbs)	Height (in)	Fat-Soluble Vitamins			Water-		
				A (mcg RE[1])	D (mcg[2])	E (mg TE[3])	C (mg)	Thiamin B-1 (mg)	Ribo-flavin B-2 (mg)
Males	11–14	99	62	1000	10	8	50	1.4	1.6
	15–18	145	69	1000	10	10	60	1.4	1.7
	19–22	154	70	1000	7.5	10	60	1.5	1.7
	23–50	154	70	1000	5	10	60	1.4	1.6
	51+	154	70	1000	5	10	60	1.2	1.4
Females	11–14	101	62	800	10	8	50	1.1	1.3
	15–18	120	64	800	10	8	60	1.1	1.3
	19–22	120	64	800	7.5	8	60	1.1	1.3
	23–50	120	64	800	5	8	60	1.0	1.2
	51+	120	64	800	5	8	60	1.0	1.2
Pregnant				+200	+5	+2	+20	+0.4	+0.3
Lactating				+400	+5	+3	+40	+0.5	+0.5

Source: Food and Nutrition Board of the National Academy of Sciences.
Note: 1 gram (g) = 1/28 ounce; 1 milligram (mg) = 1/1000 gram; 1 microgram (mcg) = 1/1,000,000 gram.

1. Vitamin A is now measured in retinol equivalents (RE). One RE equals 6 units of beta-carotene.
2. Ten mcg equal 400 international units (IU) of vitamin D.
3. Vitamin E is now measured in milligrams of tocopherol equivalents (TE).

tion. In addition, the RDA is not necessarily the amount you need every day. Rather, it's an average amount. With the body's ability to store vitamins and minerals, daily intake can vary considerably without any harmful effect on health or performance.

Using the RDAs as guidelines, numerous health organizations have analyzed the micronutrient intake of a wide variety of Americans. The Department of Agriculture and the Department of Health, Education, and Welfare both conduct periodic nutritional surveys of various income and age groups. Not surprisingly, all the

Soluble Vitamins				Minerals					
Niacin (mg NE[4])	B-6 (mg)	Folacin (mcg)	B-12 (mcg)	Calcium (mg)	Phosphorus (mg)	Magnesium (mg)	Iron (mg)	Zinc (mg)	Iodine (mcg)
18	1.8	400	3.0	1200	1200	350	18	15	150
18	2.0	400	3.0	1200	1200	400	18	15	150
19	2.2	400	3.0	800	800	350	10	15	150
18	2.2	400	3.0	800	800	350	10	15	150
16	2.2	400	3.0	800	800	350	10	15	150
15	1.8	400	3.0	1200	1200	300	18	15	150
14	2.0	400	3.0	1200	1200	300	18	15	150
14	2.0	400	3.0	800	800	300	18	15	150
13	2.0	400	3.0	800	800	300	18	15	150
13	2.0	400	3.0	800	800	300	10	15	150
+2	+0.6	+400	+1.0	+400	+400	+150	5	+5	+25
+5	+0.5	+100	+1.0	+400	+400	+150	5	+10	+50

4. Niacin is measured in milligrams of niacin equivalents (NE). One NE equals 1 mg of niacin or 60 mg of dietary tryptophan.
5. For pregnant and lactating women, iron supplements of 30–60 mg per day are recommended.

studies have shown that certain groups have special micronutrient problems: alcoholics, the chronically ill, crash-dieters, junk-food addicts, pregnant women and nursing mothers, the very poor, and the elderly. Even among these people, however, the medical problems associated with vitamin and mineral deficiencies are uncommon.

The rest of us, even on our typical American diet, fare pretty well. A sizable minority of us do seem to have trouble meeting the RDA for vitamins A and C. This is a direct result of our lack of

Estimated Safe and Adequate Daily Dietary Intakes of Selected Vitamins and Minerals[1]
(Revised 1980)

Vitamins
K: 70–140 mcg
Bitoin: 100–200 mcg
Pantothenic Acid: 4–7 mcg

Electrolytes
Sodium: 1100–3300 mg
Potassium: 1875–5625 mg
Chloride: 1700–5100 mg

Trace Elements[2]
Copper: 2.0–3.0 mg
Manganese: 2.5–5.0 mg
Fluoride: 1.5–4.0 mg
Chromium: 0.05–0.20 mg
Selenium: 0.05–0.20 mg
Molybdenum: 0.15–0.50 mg

Source: Food and Nutrition Board of the National Academy of Sciences.
Note: 1 gram (g) = 1/28 ounce; 1 milligram (mg) = 1/1000 gram; 1 microgram (mcg) = 1/1,000,000 gram

1. Because there is insufficient information on which to base allowances, these figures are not given in the table of recommended daily dietary allowances but are provided here in the form of ranges of recommended intakes.
2. Because the toxic levels for many trace elements may be only several times the usual intakes, the upper levels for the trace elements should not be habitually exceeded.

enthusiasm for vegetables and fruits. It also provides a good example for demonstrating how easy it is to meet or exceed the RDA for these two vitamins. To meet your RDA for vitamin A, forget about spinach. Don't even think about liver. Although both are excellent sources of vitamin A, both are low on most people's list of favorite foods. Instead, you can get your entire RDA for vitamin A by eating one small carrot, a few dried apricots, or half a cantaloupe. As for your RDA for vitamin C, one orange will do, or a glass of grapefruit juice, a handful of strawberries, or a serving of broccoli.

The minerals that we tend to get in short supply — calcium and iron — are more problematic. It's easy for you to satisfy the calcium RDA if you use milk and dairy products but hard if you don't. Many of us, particularly blacks, Asians, and Hispanics, can't digest the lactose in regular milk. If you can't, experiment with acidophilus milk, yogurt, buttermilk, or cottage cheese, or eat a lot of dark-

---

Iron and the Athlete

A number of studies have examined the iron needs of athletes. For the most part, the young men and women who were the subjects in these studies had adequate iron supplies. One exception was a group of endurance athletes in intensive training, who had lower than normal iron reserves but no clinical signs of iron deficiency. Usually, iron is lost only through bleeding. But the researchers speculated that these athletes were sweating so hard and so regularly that the minute amounts of iron normally lost through sweating had become cumulatively significant.

A more common iron problem among athletes is pseudoanemia. Regular exercise increases blood volume, making the concentration of red blood cells lower than in less active but statistically more average individuals. Blood tests then make it seem as if the athletes are slightly anemic, when in fact they're not.

---

green, leafy vegetables. Even if you do none of these things, however, you probably needn't worry.

Calcium deficiencies are primarily a concern for women, because they eat less and thus get less calcium in the diet, because they have less dense bone structures, because they have babies, and because they live longer. It is for these reasons that elderly women have a higher incidence of osteoporosis, the brittle-bone disease. This condition is as much a function of inactivity as of calcium intake, however, and active people — athletes, for example — are doing just what they should be doing to keep their bones strong. Osteoporosis may be aggravated by a high-protein diet, because protein decreases the absorption of calcium. Orientals, who use practically no milk or milk products but whose diet is lower in protein, rarely develop osteoporosis.

Iron too is mainly a concern for women. Because iron is lost only through bleeding, doctors are cautious about recommending iron supplements, which might gradually increase the iron store to a dangerous level. They tend to prescribe iron supplements only for pregnant women, nursing mothers, and women with heavy menstrual flows. Fortunately, to help prevent your iron reserve from becoming dangerously high, your body protects you — as it is so well equipped to do in many ways — by absorbing less iron. As with calcium and most other micronutrients, not all the iron that is in food is absorbed. Normally, the amount is less than 10 percent, and even less than this when the iron reserve is high. When it is low, the rate of absorption can triple. Absorption can also be enhanced when vitamin C is present — an example of micronutrients acting in concert.

Are there vitamins and minerals that should be of special concern to athletes? Only according to vitamin ads. An active lifestyle protects against micronutrient deficiencies by requiring the body to take in more food and by helping what is eaten to be digested and absorbed more efficiently.

Because of the enthusiasm among athletes for supplements, sports scientists have examined some of the theoretical claims for the current favorites. They have found that supplemental vitamin C won't boost endurance or speed recovery or healing; nor will vitamin E. Taking extra B vitamins for energy and stress resistance won't help either. And calcium injections aren't the answer for muscle cramps. The one category of micronutrients that active athletes should pay extra attention to is the electrolytes. But sodium, potassium, magnesium, and chlorine are among the worst candidates for supplementation. In concentrated form, they are a shock to the system — sometimes a dangerous one. Since sodium is overabundant in our diets and the other electrolytes are easily available from food, no athlete need ever incur the risks associated with taking electrolyte supplements.

One thing that most micronutrient investigators agree on is that vitamin and mineral deficiencies are at the bottom of the list of problems posed by the way we eat. Too many calories, too much fat, sugar, and salt — these are the main issues. Too little fiber, too few carbohydrates, and too much protein are next. Together, these account for virtually all the nutrition-related health problems we have. In this context, micronutrient deficiency is not only a minor matter; it is one that is automatically corrected when we work on the real problems. Thus, supplements, far from being a commonsense precaution, are really a form of pseudonutrition.

Hucksters, however, have invented the perfect diseases for pseudonutrition to treat: subclinical illnesses. They're the Catch-22s of nutrition — medical problems that cannot be detected by medical means. They supposedly plague practically all of us. The

---

The Disease That Dares Not Speak Its Name

Health and sickness are not absolute points on the continuum of human well-being. So the existence of a zone between "enough" and "not enough" micronutrients is unprovable but not implausible. If you buy the idea of subclinical deficiencies, however, you must also buy the idea of the micronutrient "diseases" that vitamin manufacturers never mention: subclinical overdoses. They are found in the gray area between "enough" and "too much" and, from a medical point of view, such "diseases" are as impossible to diagnose and treat as subclinical deficiencies. It's interesting to note that fatigue, listlessness, depression, loss of appetite, headaches, and the like also constitute the first symptoms of *excessive* micronutrient intake, as well as a whole host of problems that aren't connected with micronutrients at all. If you suffer from one of these common ailments, one or more micronutrients are unlikely culprits. But if they are, given the enrichment, fortification, and supplementation of the average American diet, a subclinical overdose is a more plausible possibility than is a subclinical deficiency.

---

most famous example from recent history is "tired blood," a condition invented so that Geritol could cure it — until the Federal Trade Commission and the courts ruled that both the disease and the cure were fictions. "Tired blood" really was a masterpiece of merchandising, however, one that exploited one of the most common and least specific signals the body can give us: fatigue.

The causes of "that run-down feeling" are as vague as the symptoms, but again, micronutrient deficiency is low on the list of possibilities. The most likely explanation for fatigue is simple inactivity. Our bodies are designed to be used, and when we feel run down, we often need to do nothing more than wind ourselves up. If you are active and feel too tired too often, you could be overtraining — not giving your body the time off that it needs to recuperate and build strength and stamina.

When there is a nutritional reason for fatigue, it is usually a lack of food energy. You aren't getting enough calories to fuel your activity level, because you are fasting, crash-dieting, or eating too much fat and protein and too little complex carbohydrate. Could you conceivably have a micronutrient deficiency? Possibly, although fatigue is also the most common symptom of a vitamin or mineral *overdose.* If you do need a micronutrient, it's probably potassium. Hardworking, hard-sweating athletes lose more potassium than other people. They need to replace this mineral regularly and can do so easily and optimally with fruits in any form.

Although advocates of micronutrient supplementation have never been able to validate any of their claims, their enthusiasm has hardly been dampened. In fact, many of them are convinced that we aren't *adequately* exceeding the RDAs. What we need, they say, are megavitamins. Megavitamins — doses at least ten times the RDA and often far more — have been hyped as panaceas for almost every serious disease and common ailment. Because the idea is attractive, megavitamins have been under intense medical scrutiny for more than a decade. The research continues, and is more than justified by the very few and very rare diseases that are helped by megavitamin therapy. Research has also shown that megadoses of micronutrients, alone or in combination, have no positive effect on any of the following: acne, arthritis, aging, autism, backache, baldness, cancer, the common cold, depression, fertility, hyperactivity, schizophrenia, sexual potency. Another important research finding has been that *megavitamins do not act as vitamins.* They function as drugs, often producing the same serious side effects. At the very least, this makes megavitamin therapy an entirely inappropriate form of self-medication.

Why do so many exaggerated and unfounded health claims for micronutrients continue to flourish in the face of all the available evidence? In part, they survive because of what is *not* known. A legitimate lack of hard scientific data allows the hucksters to palm off unfounded assumptions and conjectures as common sense. When science has demonstrated that vitamin A is essential to the normal development of the skin, it's not hard to find a handle for promoting vitamin A skin creams. So what if their effectiveness has never been proven. So what if an excess of vitamin A can cause the skin to thicken.

The same kind of connection has been made with almost every micronutrient. Shortly after a lack of vitamin E was shown to prevent reproduction in laboratory rats, the vitamin was being ballyhooed as the latest elixir of love. The claim is not very logical. Yet

Son of Tired Blood

Our nominee to succeed "tired blood" is "stress." According to almost any micronutrient ad, stress can rob the body of vitamins and minerals. As a nutritional gunslinger, however, stress is over-rated. Scientifically, stress is an extremely broad concept that covers any demand that is made on the body, and stress tolerance is an important indication of health.

Most of us regard stress in a negative way, however. We usually mean psychological stress, the kind that creates inner tensions of the sort that grind us down. Like all forms of stress, psychological stress uses energy and micronutrients. But only the most extreme forms of stress — severe injury or illness — markedly increase the need for micronutrients. Trying to deal with psychological stress by taking micronutrient supplements will give you no extra protection from the many serious stress-related diseases. Supplements may, however, help you miss the point: you must learn to manage stress with exercise, relaxation, behavior modification, and/or medication.

As for the argument that we live in uniquely stressful times and therefore need more "stress" vitamins, it can never be tested, since there is no way to quantify this kind of stress. We all yearn to live in a golden age, and perhaps most of us are convinced the present one isn't it. But would you trade rampant inflation for a rampaging woolly mammoth?

we listen. We do so for psychological rather than nutritional reasons. It's human to yearn for a shortcut, a sure thing, or a scapegoat, especially these days, when easy answers are in such short supply. Mom, apple pie, and the American way have been taking their lumps lately. Such issues as feminism, inflation, gay rights, conservation, abortion, nuclear energy, and nuclear families can be counted on to generate more heat than light. No wonder we want fast, fast, fast relief and simple solutions. Micronutrients seem to meet these needs.

It's a lot easier to take a vitamin pill than it is to take a hard look at the way we eat — and then make changes. Supplements grant the illusion of eating right, acting responsibly, and doing something good for ourselves. But they also relieve us of the burden of actually having to change. The irony is that we *can* correct the problems caused by our eating patterns, and do so far more easily than we can affect any political, social, or religious issue. We just can't do it with a pill.

Relying on a pill to solve the problem transforms nutrition from a science to a superstition. Nutritional superstitions, however appealing or comforting, leave athletes and other consumers open to exploitation. A number of words and concerns, which are discussed below, seem to suggest something about the micronutritional merits of food. But do they?

Health Foods. According to the Federal Trade Commission, the term *health food* is "undefined, undefinable, and inherently deceptive." The same can be said of most health-food stores. They are businesses, of course, designed to make money. But rare and praiseworthy are the ones that are equally devoted to sound nutrition. Most of them peddle magic in the form of products with few, if any, nutritional advantages and greatly inflated prices. Happily, most supermarkets now stock whole grains, wheat germ, bean curd, seeds, sprouts, and similar foods that were once available only in specialty stores at premium prices. The producers of these items are careful to maintain their health-food aura, which is why we see Soviet Georgian geriatrics gobbling Dannon yogurt. Although yogurt is in no way superior to the milk from which it is made (except in price), it is a nutritious and useful food. It won't work wonders, but no food will.

Natural. The label *natural* is used for foods that have been minimally processed and that contain no preservatives and no artificial ingredients. But it has been applied so loosely that it says nothing about the nutritional value of a food. "Natural" breakfast foods are loaded with sugar, "natural" potato chips with salt and fat, "natural" beers with additives. All have been processed to a fare-thee-well. "Natural" vitamins are manufactured, not harvested. Frequently, they are partly or mostly synthetic — vitamin C "with rose hips," for example, derives only a small percentage of its vitamin C from rose hips. Even all-natural micronutrients are chemically identical to their synthetic counterparts. "Natural" vitamins are hazardous to your budget; your body won't know the difference.

Organic. The term *organic* should refer to food grown without chemical fertilizers and pesticides. Organic farming is neither eccentric nor inefficient, but organically grown foods have no nutritional advantages. Plants can absorb nutrients from the soil only in inorganic form, and they don't care if these nutrients have been supplied by manure or by chemical fertilizers. Even worn-out soil affects only the amount, not the nutritional value, of what manages to grow in it. The only disease that has been traceable to a deficiency in soil is simple goiter, which has been eliminated by the addition of a minute amount of iodine to table salt.

Pesticides, Antibiotics, and Hormones. In recent years, concern has been expressed about the use of pesticides, antibiotics, and hormones in our food sources. They don't affect the micronutrient content of foods, but they do increase the yield in conventional, large-scale farming. However, traces of pesticides do end up in human tissues, as do traces of antibiotics and growth hormones used in animal feed. No study has connected these substances with health problems, but they nevertheless merit our concern. Significantly, most comparisons of organic and nonorganic produce have revealed about the same trace levels of pesticides, which can drift from neighboring farms, settle into the water table, and linger in the soil for years. Washing produce helps. So does limiting the intake of animal fat, which is most likely to contain these substances.

Processing. All forms of processing result in a loss of micronutrients. This is an extremely minor matter when fresh and lightly processed foods are favored. Although canned and frozen fruits and vegetables commonly lose a third of their micronutrients in processing, they are still good sources of vitamins and minerals.

A lot of our food has been so overprocessed that far too many micronutrients have been lost. Supplementation is one answer to this problem. But it can't compensate for the fat, sugar, and salt that are the predominant additives in overprocessed food. A far better solution is to use foods that have not been overprocessed. They are cheaper, tastier, and more nutritious than the combination of overprocessed foods and supplements.

Some kinds of processing have been promoted as superior to others. Stone-ground flour may have a preferable texture and taste, but it has no nutritional benefit. It's the refining, not the grinding, that counts. *Cold-pressed* (which refers to one way that vegetable oils can be extracted) is an inaccurate and meaningless term and doesn't signify a nutritional advantage. Taste and price are the only factors that need be considered in buying vegetable oils. Pasteurization, a breakthrough of the nineteenth century, protects us from diseases like tuberculosis and undulant fever, whose causative organisms can be carried by raw milk. The process destroys a little vitamin C (which is not the nutrient we expect to get from milk anyway) but preserves the quality of the protein. Certified raw milk is an expensive, unpasteurized, high-priced alternative. It's safe, although from time to time batches have been linked to cases of salmonella food poisoning.

Additives. Thousands of flavorings, emulsifiers, stabilizers, acidulants, and preservatives are added to foods. Most of them appear on the Generally Recognized as Safe (GRAS) list of the Food and Drug Administration. Some of them are foods (sugar, salt, vinegar) or are found in food (vegetable proteins, micronutrients). Calcium propionate, for example, which retards the formation of mold on bread, has a forbidding-sounding name, but it occurs naturally in raisins and Swiss cheese. By and large, additives are safe and useful for increasing the stability and shelf life of many nutritious foods. On the other hand, reading a Cool Whip, Tang, or Cup-a-Soup label may make you wonder where the food went. So the questions are, Which additives are acceptable, and in what amounts?

The additives that create the greatest concern and controversy are sugar and salt, but there are others. Large doses of saccharin and sodium nitrite (a preservative in cured meats, such as bacon) have been shown to cause cancer in laboratory animals. BHT, BHA, and propyl gallate are preservatives of dubious value. EDTA, calcium phytate, and sodium phosphate can bind to calcium and iron, preventing their absorption. Food colorings are entirely cosmetic. Without coloring, oranges are not that orange, margarine isn't yellow, and hot dogs aren't pink. Studies have shown a link between eye appeal and taste appeal. And the food industry claims that we won't buy foods that don't look the way it has persuaded us they ought to, so they continue to alter the color of many of the things we eat.

Micronutrients are used to enrich (replace nutrients lost in processing) or fortify (add new nutrients) a staggering variety of foods. They are probably harmless. But are they effective? The fortification and enrichment of basic foods have succeeded in virtually eliminating vitamin-deficiency diseases. But the addition of micronutrients in processing can give a false impression of a food's value. For example, one of the highest-ranked breakfast cereals in a *Consumer Reports* comparison study was an old standby: unfortified, unsalted, unsugared Nabisco Shredded Wheat. Among the lowest ranked were three of the most fortified and most expensive: Total, Most, and Product 19. On the other hand, a *Consumer Reports* test of breads has shown that fortified white bread isn't nutritionally inferior to unfortified whole-wheat bread, except in fiber content. Fortification isn't a guarantee that vitamins and minerals will be absorbed and used. Absorption and utilization are determined by many factors, including the way the food has been processed and whether other nutrients are present or absent. Nor does the addition of micronutrients to foods that are high in fat, sugar, and salt do anything to offset these more serious drawbacks. Fruit drinks to which vitamin C has been added, for example, are loaded with empty calories from sugar, and they lack a variety of important nutrients found in fresh fruits and their juices.

None of this is an argument for an additive-free diet, an expensive and unnecessary precaution requiring extraordinary vigilance. As with every other aspect of nutrition, however, moderation, balance, and variety are virtues. So are labeling laws. An easy way for us to reduce our additive intake dramatically is to read labels and avoid the foods that contain too many things whose names we can't pronounce (see chapter 13).

Food Preparation. As with processing, the preparation of food causes micronutrients to be lost. Yet cooking also destroys toxins, parasites, and bacteria and makes meats and grains more digestible. Nutrient loss is of greatest concern with fruits and vegetables, which are rich in the water-soluble vitamins, B complex and C. These vitamins are the least efficiently stored vitamins, and it's best to get them regularly. Fresh produce, however, can lose vitamins during preparation. (Chapter 14 suggests a number of cooking strategies designed to minimize this loss.)

Fast Foods, Junk Foods, and Food Fads. One of every three American meals falls into the fast-food category. With their added fat, sugar, and salt, most fast foods offer fewer micronutrients per calorie than less processed foods. But fast foods aren't junk foods either. At least the burgers, chicken, fish, pizza, and sandwiches aren't. (If you spend a lot of time in the fast-food lane, however, be sure to read chapter 15.)

Junk foods are defended by no one yet eaten by everyone. Strict constructionists limit the term to foods that are high in calories and low in nutrients. The classic candidates are candy and soft drinks, which are closely followed by most sweets and desserts. Breakfast cereals with the sugar content of candy can also be listed. Although it's true that ice cream is a lot more nutritious than chocolate fudge, this fact is misleading, because it misses the point: a day-to-day diet of junk foods will fatten us. If it doesn't, that's because the junk foods are taking the place of more nutritious foods. Treat junk foods as a treat — as a sometime thing.

Perhaps the most effective eating methods that reduce our micronutrient intake are crash-dieting, fasting, and skipping meals. In the process we also reduce our energy level. This is a problem that supplements can't correct. *Because vitamins and minerals have no calories, they are not sources of energy.* Athletes cannot maintain high energy on a low-calorie diet, no matter how high their micronutrient intake. Athletes can, however, maintain their desired weight, or level of body fat, and high energy by combining high activity with a moderate number of calories obtained regularly throughout the day.

Food fads can also affect the amounts of micronutrients we get. The potential problem is that they render the nutritional value of food secondary to psychological or spiritual values. Vegetarianism, the world's first food fad, is based on beliefs that the body is poorly suited to the consumption of animal foods, that eating them produces animalistic behavior, and that eating only plant foods will put people in greater harmony with nature. These variations of "you are what you eat" have no scientific basis. Even so, a vegetarian diet is better than the average American diet, because it is generally lower in calories and fat and higher in complex carbohydrates, fiber, and many micronutrients. The only vitamin deficiency that strict vegetarians can — but seldom do — encounter is a deficiency of vitamin B-12, which only animal foods contain.

Other food fads are downright dangerous, because they are radically unbalanced. High-protein, low-carbohydrate diets can dehydrate the body and rob it of energy. However, you probably wouldn't be able to stay on one long enough to threaten your micronutrient supply. The same may not be true of the Beverly Hills diet, which is restricted to huge amounts of fruits in a specific sequence. This foolish diet is dangerously low in protein and many micronutrients, often causes diarrhea, and definitely drains the wallet. The most limited, and therefore most dangerous, diets of recent times are the liquid-protein diet and the brown-rice diet, both of which have caused a number of deaths.

The best of the current batch of fad diets is the Pritikin diet. Designed as a nutritional treatment for people with serious heart disease, it drastically restricts fat, cholesterol, sugar, and salt; limits meat; and includes lots of fruits, vegetables, and whole grains. Its main nutritional drawback is that it may produce a minor deficiency of fatty acids. Its advantages have yet to be scientifically demonstrated. The problem with this diet is a practical one: because it departs so dramatically from typical eating patterns, it is demanding and difficult to follow. The Intensive Training plan described in chapters 3 and 12 is simpler but almost as extreme and can therefore be considered a temporary, "crashless" diet.

Absorption. For what we eat to do us any good, it has to get into our system. The absorption of micronutrients is decreased by any of a number of factors, including inactivity, gastrointestinal disorders, diarrhea, laxatives, poor eating patterns, and a surplus of stored micronutrients. Absorption is greater when we are active, when we eat a balanced diet, or when our micronutrient reserves are on the low side and need replenishing. Supplements taken without food are poorly absorbed, but better absorbed when taken with foods in which they are naturally found. The absorption issue is a complicated one. For active athletes — even those with poor eating habits — it's not worth worrying about.

Supplements. It has long been an article of faith that vitamin and mineral pills are safe. No one wants us to believe this more than the people who promote, and profit from, their sale. Indeed, safety has been one of the arguments used to counter the government's attempts to regulate the sale of supplements. The truth is that their safety has often been disproven in megadoses and has never been demonstrated in lesser overdoses.

If you are self-dosing with an all-in-one tablet, you're probably exceeding your RDA of each nutrient it contains by 100 percent or more. You have a good idea of what 100 percent more fat, sugar, salt, or protein would mean. But you'll probably never know whether 100 percent more than the RDA of micronutrients is an excessive overdose. Life outside the laboratory is complex and un-

The Most Dangerous Micronutrient

In ancient times, salt was a preservative, a flavoring, and a commodity whose worth was enhanced by its scarcity. Today salt is cheap and plentiful, which may help to explain why we are dangerously exceeding our need for this substance.

Salt (sodium chloride) is the most common source of sodium in our diet. Excessive sodium is a serious health problem because one in five of us is predisposed to high blood pressure, and a high-salt diet can trigger that predisposition. In Japan, with the highest per capita salt consumption in the world, high blood pressure is the leading cause of death. In societies with low salt consumption, hypertension is not a problem.

Unfortunately, there is no way to predict which of us will develop hypertension. By the time it is diagnosed, some damage has already been done. Hypertension is, however, the most treatable serious disease. In borderline cases, a low-salt diet alone is sufficient. But health officials point out that it is easier and healthier to moderate our salt intake before we have to.

This sensible advice is not as simple to follow as it sounds, because we don't control two-thirds of the salt we consume. The food industry does. In most cases, it uses salt to add flavor to foods that have lost their flavor in processing. But many foods, such as cottage cheese, cereals, and puddings, can contain a fair amount of salt without tasting salty. Without labeling laws for sodium content, the only practical way to cut your salt intake is to reduce your dependency on the canned, frozen, and fast foods that contain excessive amounts of salt.

controllable. Designing a study that would effectively isolate the effect of one or more micronutrients in the diet is impossible. Even so, what is known about these substances is important in reaching an informed decision about supplements:

1. Micronutrient deficiencies are not a significant nutritional issue for most of us.

2. The body is ideally equipped to derive all its nutrients from the foods in which they naturally occur.

3. There is no evidence that exceeding the RDA for any micronutrient is beneficial.

4. The functions of micronutrients are numerous and imperfectly understood. It is known, however, that they are interactive and interdependent and that supplements can upset their balance.

5. Overdoses are riskiest for pregnant women, nursing mothers, and growing children.

6. Vitamins A, D, and K (three of the fat-soluble vitamins) and most minerals are stored in the body, so toxic overdoses are possible. (Vitamin E, the other fat-soluble vitamin, can also be stored, but it's hard to overdose.)

7. The water-soluble vitamins (the B complex and C) and some minerals are easily excreted in the urine. Although dangerous overdoses are uncommon, megadoses sometimes cause trouble just passing through the system.

8. Overdoses of some micronutrients can interfere with medications and cause false readings on blood and urine tests.

9. The most easily demonstrated effect of overdosing is a placebo effect (see chapter 11).

Thanks to vitamin and mineral supplements, the United States has the highest micronutrient intake in the world. The benefits, however, are not apparent. We are not an unhealthy nation, but the national health in such places as Japan and most of Western Europe, where there is no mania for micronutrients, is somewhat better than ours. American athletes are among the biggest users and boosters of supplements. Has it earned them anything more than the honor of having the most expensive urine in the world? In world-class competition, even the smallest competitive edge should show. But, as well as this country does, it doesn't dominate the world of sports. No nation does. To make an informed decision about micronutrients, you would want scientific evidence that extra amounts promote performance. But there isn't any evidence. What you should do is treat the issue of vitamins and minerals as any average athlete with normal eating patterns can: as a non-issue.

Facts about Micronutrients

Nutrient	Some Major Functions	Risk of Not Meeting RDA
Fat-soluble vitamins		
A (retinol)	Maintains vision, skin, mucous membranes, and resistance to infection	Moderate, but easily corrected
D	Builds bones and teeth by aiding calcium absorption	Unlikely
E	Poorly understood. Important as an antioxidant in energy metabolism; spares or protects vitamin A	Unlikely
K	Involved in blood clotting	Unlikely
Water-soluble vitamins		
B-1 (thiamine)	The B-complex are cofactors in the metabolism of food. They are so closely interrelated that inadequate or excessive intake of one may impair the utilization of others.	Low
B-2 (riboflavin)		Low
Niacin		Unlikely
B-6 (pyridoxone)		Unlikely (high-protein diet and oral contraceptives increase need slightly)

Sources	Signs and Symptoms of Deficiency	Signs and Symptoms of Overdose
Fortified milk, carrots, apricots, cantaloupes, green leafy vegetables	Night blindness, dry rough skin	Night blindness, dry rough skin (same as for deficiency)
Fortified milk Sunshine	Rickets (crippling bone deformities)	Mental or physical retardation, abnormal heartbeat, vomiting, constipation, kidney damage
Vegetable oils, margarines, grains, fish	None known	Increased need for vitamins A, D, and K, abnormal blood clotting
Green vegetables, liver, coffee	Severe bleeding	Inhibition of liver bile excretion, ruptured red blood cells
The B-complex are easily available in a wide variety of plant and animal foods, including meats, grains, beans, vegetables.	Beriberi (swollen limbs, edema, emaciation)	None known
	Reddened lips, cracks at corner of mouth, eye lesions	None known
	Pellagra (skin lesions, mental disorders)	Flushing, burning, or tingling of skin; rash, nausea, diarrhea, activation of peptic ulcers
	Irritability, convulsions, kidney stones	Liver damage, vitamin dependency

Nutrient	Some Major Functions	Risk of Not Meeting RDA
Water-soluble vitamins		
Pantothenic acid		Unlikely
Folacin		Unlikely
B-12		Unlikely
Biotin		Unlikely
C (ascorbic acid)	Maintains collagen (a kind of cell "glue") and resistance to infection	Moderate, but easily corrected
Minerals		
Calcium	Builds bones and teeth	Moderate when milk and dairy products are not in the diet
Phosphorus	Builds bones and teeth; metabolism	Unlikely

Sources	Signs and Symptoms of Deficiency	Signs and Symptoms of Overdose
	Fatigue, depression, confusion	Diarrhea
	Anemia, stunted growth, intestinal damage	
	Pernicious anemia	Nervous system damage
	Skin inflammation, hair loss, fatigue, depression	None known
Citrus fruits, peppers, most other fruits and vegetables	Scurvy (degeneration of skin, teeth, gums, and blood vessels)	Vitamin dependency, diarrhea, crystals in urine, kidney stones, abnormal vitamin B-12 utilization
Milk and dairy products; leafy green vegetables	Osteoporosis	Abnormal absorption of other minerals, calcium deposits in soft tissues
Protein-rich foods (meat, fish, milk and dairy products, beans, grains), carbonated drinks	Prolonged use of antacids will create a deficiency.	Abnormal calcium–phosphorus balance

Nutrient	Some Major Functions	Risk of Not Meeting RDA
Minerals		
Magnesium	Builds bones and muscles; energy use	Unlikely
Sodium	Sodium, potassium, and chlorine are intimately related in the maintenance of fluid levels and muscular contractions.	Unlikely
Potassium		Unlikely
Chlorine*		Unlikely
Sulfur	Energy use; works with vitamin B-1 and biotin	Unlikely
Iron	Oxygen transport	Unlikely, except moderate in menstruating, pregnant, or nursing women
Zinc	Tissue growth; gonadal development	Unlikely
Copper	Formation of hemoglobin; affects iron absorption	Unlikely

Sources	Signs and Symptoms of Deficiency	Signs and Symptoms of Overdose
Grains, nuts, meats, beans	Loss of body fluids, hormone or kidney problems, abnormal mineral balance	Diarrhea, abnormal mineral balance
Table salt; small amounts in most foods except fruits	A deficiency of sodium, potassium, or chlorine can cause fatigue, weakness, irritability, loss of appetite, nausea, cramps, mental confusion.	Hypertension, fluid retention, kidney problems
Avocados, apricots, bananas, peanuts, milk, meat, fruits, vegetables		Kidney problems, acidosis, irregular heartbeat
Table salt, seafood, milk, meat, eggs		Not clear because of its intimate connection with sodium intake
Protein-rich foods	None known	None known
Meat, eggs, beans, grains, dark green vegetables, shellfish	Anemia (pallor, fatigue, mouth soreness)	Heart, liver, or pancreas damage
Milk, liver, shellfish, wheat bran, eggs	Loss of taste, mimics vitamin A deficiency	Iron depletion
Liver, shellfish, whole grains, legumes, nuts, dried fruits	Anemia	Nausea, headache, fatigue

Nutrient	Some Major Functions	Risk of Not Meeting RDA
Minerals		
Iodine	Formation of compounds secreted by the thyroid gland	Unlikely
Manganese	Bone and tissue development and fat synthesis	Unlikely
Fluorine	Formation of bones and tooth enamel	Unlikely

Sermonette

Life is often incongruous. And everyone has to make a living. So we've resigned ourselves to the fact that major sporting events are backed by tobacco companies. We can also live with the endless stream of ads featuring professional jocks guzzling soft drinks and beer. (At least they don't directly equate refreshment with nutrition and fitness.) But we are downright cranky on the subject of champion athletes and the trainers of champions who promote vitamin and mineral supplements. So they take the pills they endorse. So they are only expressing the same misconceptions about micronutrients that most Americans hold. So they're making a pretty penny from their endorsements. So maybe it's unrealistic to expect them to consider the athletes, including you, at whom these ads are aimed. Ninety-nine percent of you will never earn a nickel from your sport. What we have here is the exploitation of amateur athletes by professional athletes — who ought to know better.

Vitamins and minerals are essential to health and performance, but supplements are, at best, unnecessary and expensive. They cannot substitute for the eating patterns you need to develop to fuel your training, eating patterns that are abundantly rich in all micronutrients. Nor can supplements protect you from the serious ways in which poor eating patterns can undermine your energy.

Sources	Signs and Symptoms of Deficiency	Signs and Symptoms of Overdose
Iodized salt, sea-food	Goiter (enlarged thyroid)	None known
Nuts, grains, beans, tea, fruits, vegetables	None known	Weakness, motor difficulties, impairment of iron absorption
Tap water, tea, coffee, rice, spinach, onions, lettuce	Excessive tooth decay	Stained teeth; growth retardation

11

The Dilemma of Drugs

Competitions in sports must not be allowed to become competitions between pharmacologists and physicians using competitors as guinea pigs.

ARNOLD BECKETT
Medical Controls, 21st Olympiad, 1976

Perhaps the greatest challenge of all, today, is to get across to people that the so-called "drugs" used in sports activities have *absolutely no justifiable role in athletics*, for they dim perception and judgment, and dull skilled performance. Stimulants, depressants, strength- and muscle-building steroids, diuretics, strong pain-killers — all have been found to be of no value in sports.

JOSEPH D. GODFREY
American Journal of Sports Medicine

A few years ago I polled more than a hundred top runners and posed this question: "If I could give you a pill that would make you an Olympic champion — and also kill you in a year — would you take it?" To my amazement, more than half of the athletes responding stated that they would take my magic pill. It is this attitude that explains why drug-taking is such a monumental problem in sports today.

GABE MIRKIN
The Sportsmedicine Book

"HERE," SAYS THE GODDESS, bending over the fallen warrior, "drink this." He does, and then he leaps back into the fray, refreshed and rejuvenated. Every age and culture has a version of this myth, in which strength, spirits, and energy are restored by a mysterious potion.

We're no different in our desire for a magic elixir. But we are unique in having an unparalleled number of supposedly potent potions to choose from. Strictly speaking, these substances don't belong in a book on optimal nutrition, because they aren't nutrients. However, most athletes have used one or more drugs, hoping to increase strength, stamina, and skill or to decrease discomfort. Like protein and micronutrients, drugs have an aura of ergogenic magic about them. For this reason, a close look at their benefits and risks is warranted.

Drugs are as common in sports as they are in society at large, and involve the same moral, ethical, and legal considerations. The dilemma of drugs is further complicated by psychological factors. The urge to excel is a powerful one. So are the desires to be a team player and to live up to the expectations of teammates, coaches, parents, friends, and fans. As the stakes go up, so do these pressures, and the need to win becomes the need to win at any price. The promise of drugs is that they will help athletes win. Whatever the price, though, it's the athlete who pays.

The following information should tell you what price you're likely to pay and what benefits you're likely to gain. A few non-drugs (e.g., oxygen) and one technique (blood boosting) are included because they are approached and used with the same expectations. (Amphetamines and steroids, the most potent and most misunderstood drugs commonly used by athletes, are discussed later in separate sections.)

Adrenaline. See *Epinephrine.*

Alcohol. Our most popular legal recreational drug. Widely — and wrongly — regarded as a stimulant because it initially reduces inhibitions, alcohol actually depresses the central nervous system. As a result, alertness, judgment, coordination, and reflexes are impaired. Alcohol also greatly promotes fatigue by slowing the removal of lactic acid from cells. (It's the accumulation of lactic acid in the muscles that produces fatigue in the first place.) In addition, alcohol dehydrates and reduces heat tolerance.

Antacids. Substances that neutralize acids. Some athletes believe that since exercise causes the formation of lactic acid, and lactic acid produces fatigue, the way to combat fatigue is to take an antacid to buffer or neutralize the acid. They're wrong. The buffering process, which occurs naturally as the alkali reserves in the blood are drawn on, cannot be hastened by taking an antacid in pill form.

Analgesics. Drugs that relieve pain — including aspirin, aspirin substitutes (such as Tylenol), Butazolidin, and narcotics, all of which are discussed below.

Playing on Painkillers

It's the last period of the all-state finals. We're behind, but we've got the momentum — and now the ball. A flurry of activity. Score! But wait. One of our players is down. Oh, no, it's Garrett, the best all-round athlete Central High has seen in years. And it looks as if she's out of the game. The team doctor hustles over to examine her knee. Nothing broken. Probably just some sprained ligaments. Now the doctor, the coach, the team, the family, the fans — all are staring at Garrett with one thought: Can she play? No one wants this victory more than she does. If they can just give her something for the pain . . .

This is a commonplace scenario in competitive sports, and it illustrates the problem with painkillers: when athletes need them most, they are least able to make an informed decision. They will want to play at almost any cost. If you're like this, the most sensible decision you can make about playing on painkillers is the one you make before you need them.

Pain is a warning message from the body to pay attention, and successful athletes have learned how to do just that. They know when pain can be worked through, and when it must be respected. Rather than ignore pain, they monitor it. Painkillers short-circuit this process. By masking the pain, they make it possible to play on. But when athletes cannot play without painkillers, they are already injured. And when they can play without feeling pain, the risk of further injury increases substantially.

If you are involved in sports for personal satisfaction, it's hard to imagine a benefit worth the risk of playing on painkillers. If you're

---

in pain, lighten the load, ease the pace, and try aspirin. And start warming up religiously. This simple form of preventive medicine dramatically reduces athletic injuries. If you aren't mending, find a doctor who specializes in sports medicine, and consider the cost an investment for the long run.

If you are in organized sports, ask yourself the following: Are you *that* important to your team's success? Will this game affect your future? Will the outcome make much difference this time next season? Is your coach a trained expert as well as an enthusiast? Is there a team physician? Do you have confidence in him or her? Do you think he or she is knowledgeable about sports medicine? Do you know of any facilities near you that specialize in assessing, treating, and preventing sports injuries? If you came up with "no" answers, you're missing the kind of insurance that reduces the risks of playing on painkillers.

Aspirin. Our oldest wonder drug. Inexpensive and available without a prescription, aspirin reduces pain, swelling, and fever. Even a normal dose (10 grains) or less, taken every four hours for twenty-four hours or less, may cause mild stomach upset. This side effect can be avoided by taking aspirin with milk or by using a time-released, buffered, or coated form. (Coated forms pass through the stomach before the coating dissolves.) If aspirin doesn't relieve your pain, see a doctor. Some competitive runners use aspirin to run "cooler," but this practice can be dangerous, for aspirin can predispose to heat illness by increasing sweating, inhibiting the sense of thirst, and blunting the sense of fatigue.

Barbiturates (also known as downers and soapers — from *soporific*, which means "sleep inducing"). Drugs that depress the central nervous system, inhibiting muscle activity and decreasing oxygen consumption. For this reason, barbiturates are not used in competition but are taken afterward by some athletes to counteract the effects of amphetamines. In low doses, barbiturates act as sedatives, but they do not relieve pain. Because they lose their effectiveness if used often and because frequent use increases the risks for psychological and physical dependency as well as for addiction, an increasing number of doctors are refusing to prescribe them.

Barbiturates are especially dangerous in combination with alcohol.

Bee pollen. Bee food — a combination of nectar and pollen. According to its proponents, bee pollen increases strength, stamina, speed, and recovery rate. Scientists who have conducted controlled studies find that it does none of these things. It's reasonably nutritious, but it doesn't contain anything that can't be obtained from less exotic items with far less exotic prices.

Beta-blockers. Drugs that are used to control blood pressure and that in higher doses have proven of limited usefulness in treating severe anxiety in performers and public speakers. In a small-scale experiment with Finnish ski jumpers that was designed to test whether beta-blockers improve concentration, timing, judgment, and thus performance, the results were inconclusive; however, some jumpers reported numbness and nausea. Other tests have shown that beta-blockers do not improve the efficiency of the heart or lungs.

"Vitamin B-15" ("pangamic acid"). According to the Food and Drug Administration, "not an identifiable substance." The chemical composition varies from product to product. Most often, it is a mix of sodium gluconate or calcium gluconate, glycine, and dichloroacetate (one of a family of chemicals that are known carcinogens). The agency also finds that there is "no accepted scientific evidence establishing any nutritional properties . . . or other usefulness" for such substances. As a result, the preparations have been banned from the mails.

Blood boosting (also known as blood doping and blood infusion). A technique that supposedly increases the amount of oxygen that can be transported by the blood. It involves drawing a pint of blood five to six weeks before the big race. The red blood cells are centrifuged out of this pint and stored. Over the next four weeks, the body replaces the lost red blood cells. A week before the race, the red blood cells that have been removed and stored are reinfused. Thus, the number of these oxygen carriers is increased. Even in highly trained runners, however, this has been shown to increase oxygen intake and endurance only slightly or not at all. The process may also thicken the blood, making it harder to pump through the small arteries.

Butazolidin (phenylbutazone; also known as bute). Reduces pain associated with inflammation more rapidly and effectively than aspirin. Butazolidin is also more toxic, and it has a number of unpleasant side effects, such as ulcers, rashes, water retention, internal bleeding, and anemia. More significantly, large doses reduce pain so effectively that injured athletes are able to continue playing, often with disastrous consequences.

Caffeine. The most widely consumed of all stimulants, caffeine occurs in coffee, tea, cola drinks, cocoa, No-Doz, and several headache medications. It does not rate high marks from nutritionists or the medical community, in part because it has joined the ranks of common substances such as alcohol and tobacco that are suspected or known to increase the risk of birth defects and cancer. In people with a low tolerance for, or little experience with, caffeine, it can produce queasiness or jitters ("coffee nerves") and even imitate the symptoms of anxiety. This gives it the potential to interfere with concentration and coordination. Caffeine is also habit forming, which is why millions of us don't feel up to par until we've gotten our morning jolt from coffee — and why Hugh Hefner was once addicted to Pepsi. Caffeine is also a diuretic, a substance that increases urination and thus promotes dehydration, which is an important consideration in hot weather.

Nevertheless, caffeine has gained a reputation as an endurance enhancer. In a study of trained cyclists, 250 milligrams of caffeine (about two and a half cups of brewed coffee) an hour prior to performance plus another 250 milligrams over the next ninety minutes increased the amount of work that could be done in a two-hour cycling exercise by 7 percent. For the first fifty minutes, caffeine only stimulates the central nervous system, lowering the perception of exertion. After that, it seems to have a glycogen-sparing effect by increasing the rate at which fat is burned. These findings explain why there is plenty of experimentation with caffeine going on among top-level endurance athletes. And perhaps because caffeine is so commonly used and because its risks are so minor when compared with those of other stimulants, there has yet been no cry of caffeine abuse.

Cocaine. A "relatively safe" stimulant. Unlike narcotics, cocaine is not addictive, but it is habit forming, as numerous professional athletes (members of one of the few groups with incomes high enough to be able to abuse this outrageously expensive drug) can attest. Its impact on the central nervous system is somewhat similar to that of amphetamines, but its effect is more immediate and much less sustained. Consequently, cocaine makes athletes feel better, but it doesn't enable them to play better.

Cortisone and other corticoids (also known as corticosteroids). Some of the many hormones secreted by the adrenal glands; not to be confused with anabolic steroids. Cortisone relieves stress, fatigue, and inflammation resulting from hard physical exertion. The adrenal glands stop producing cortisone soon after synthetic cortisone is introduced into the body, and are slow to resume production after synthetic cortisone use stops. Synthetic corticoids elevate mood, increase the pain threshold, and reduce inflammation. Side effects from extended use include stomach problems, osteoporosis, prostatitis, and urinary infections. Prolonged usage results in Cushing's syndrome, marked by fluid retention, elevated appetite, "moon face," skin lesions, and euphoria. In 1977, cyclist Bernard Thevet, twice the winner of the Tour de France, was forced into premature retirement. He blamed it on failing health caused by cortisone and its severe effects on his adrenal glands. (Safe and effective cortisone creams for minor skin irritations are now sold without prescription.)

Digitalis. A heart stimulant made from the dried leaves of foxglove and traditionally used by people with coronary heart disease. Digitalis makes the heart race, but it won't make you race any faster or farther.

DMSO (dimethyl sulfoxide). A controversial, anti-inflammatory salve for treating sprains, bruises, tendonitis, shin splints, and torn muscles. Many athletes and trainers consider DMSO a wonder drug. Doctors and researchers are less convinced that it is any more effective than other forms of treatment. DMSO was developed as an industrial solvent and paint thinner. Veterinarians use it to treat inflammation in horses and dogs. The Food and Drug Administration, however, has cleared DMSO for human use only in the treatment of a certain type of cystitis. Repeated high doses have caused eye damage and birth defects in laboratory animals. Its long-term risks to humans are unknown, but occasional side effects are skin burns and allergic reactions. DMSO's universal drawback, however, is its ferocious smell, both in the bottle and in the body. It causes what some athletes call "death breath."

Diuretics. Drugs that increase urination. Diuretics are used medically to treat sodium retention and hypertension. They are used by athletes who must lose weight fast before weighing in.

This form of deliberate dehydration negatively affects muscular strength, blood plasma and blood volume, heart function, oxygen consumption, heat regulation, blood flow to the kidneys, liver glycogen, and electrolyte balance. In studies of healthy, young wrestlers, the cardiovascular effects largely disappeared when there was free access to fluids between weigh-in and competition. But this kind of rapid weight loss always compromises strength and energy.

Ephedrine. A mild stimulant that dilates the breathing passages and relieves congestion; widely used in over-the-counter allergy and asthma medications. Because ephedrine affects the central nervous system, it may cause such side effects as sleeplessness, restlessness, and nervousness. In the 1890s, a British cyclist using ephedrine crashed and died, becoming the first recorded death from drug use in sports. At the 1972 Olympics in Munich, American swimmer Rick DeMont lost his gold medal when ephedrine from his asthma medication showed up in his blood test. Subsequent studies have shown that therapeutic doses of ephedrine have no effect on exercise capacity, lung function, or overall performance.

Epinephrine. A hormone produced by the adrenal glands that prepares the body for action by stimulating the heart, constricting the blood vessels, and opening the breathing passages. Taken in synthetic form in the belief that it will even better prepare the body for action, epinephrine's effects can be felt, but they are not ergogenic.

Marijuana. Our most popular illegal recreational drug. Marijuana contains a mild narcotic that distorts perception and affects mood. In short, it adversely affects performance, but the smoker won't care. It also has the same detrimental impact on oxygen consumption that nicotine has.

Narcotics. A group of painkillers including opium, codeine and morphine (constituents of opium), and heroin (a derivative of morphine). The fact that narcotics are powerfully addictive is reason enough to avoid them. When used under medical supervision, they can be useful for relieving pain by depressing the central nervous system and thereby numbing the senses and inducing sleep. Athletes who use narcotics won't hurt — they won't want to play either.

Meperidrine (Demerol) and propoxyphene (Darvon), synthetic narcoticlike painkillers, are also addictive. And Darvon, in fact, has been shown to be less effective than aspirin.

Nicotine. A toxic alkaloid found in tobacco. Nicotine constricts blood vessels, raises blood pressure, and increases heart rate — none of which helps performance.

Novocaine. See *Procaine.*

Oxygen. Inhaling pure oxygen increases the oxygen level in the blood, but the effect is extremely brief. Since the body cannot store oxygen, the only time that inhaling oxygen might benefit an athlete is during performance. Doing so after performing does not speed the elimination of such by-products as lactic acid.

Placebo. An extremely effective drug substitute: a nondrug substance (such as a sugar pill) that is routinely used in scientific double-blind studies. Placebos demonstrate the truth of mind over matter. Like Dumbo with his magic feather, if we are told or if we believe that a substance will improve our performance or decrease our pain, it probably will, even if what we're given is a sugar pill. We feel what we expect to feel, which is why our mental attitude and expectations have such a profound effect on how we perform. Everyone "knows" that amphetamines provide a psychological boost, giving a sense of increased alertness. But twenty years ago, before this "fact" had become so firmly established, a test of twenty athletes showed otherwise. Ten were given amphetamines, ten a placebo. Only *one* athlete correctly identified which one he received. The other nineteen either thought they had gotten speed when they hadn't, or thought they hadn't when they had.

The people who profit most from the placebo effect are the merchandisers of all the nutritional supplements and pills that, at one time or another, we've all been persuaded to buy. Once we started taking them, we began to experience a very human need — the need to persuade ourselves that we had made a wise investment — and protected ourselves from any evidence to the contrary. This is one way in which something worthless can wind up working, at least for a while. It puts a dent in our self-esteem to admit that we've been had. But there's something worse: to continue being had.

Procaine. A widely used painkiller marketed under such trade names as Novocaine and Xylocaine. You get Novocaine from your dentist, so you know how well it works. An athlete injured in team play who wants nothing more than to continue playing will probably get procaine from the team doctor, because it won't turn the mind to mush, as many other painkillers will. It will, however, greatly increase the chance that you will aggravate your injury.

Thyroid (thyroxine). A hormone produced by the thyroid gland that regulates metabolism. Some athletes — notably Muhammad Ali, before the title fight that effectively ended his career — have used thyroid extracts in the hope of accelerating weight loss. But the amount of extra thyroid it takes to burn fat faster also erodes muscle strength, throws off the normal biochemical balance of the system, and causes such side effects as dizziness, spasms, and jitters.

Tranquilizers. Drugs that calm the central nervous system and reduce tension. Like the best-known brand, Valium, all other tranquilizers are habit forming, and they become decreasingly effective when used regularly. Tranquilizers are sometimes prescribed as mild muscle relaxants. Doctors will tell athletes to use them after the game, however, because tranquilizers are sedatives. Although they don't affect alertness as much as barbiturates and narcotics do, they do affect frame of mind.

Tylenol (acetaminophen). The best-known brand of aspirin substitute. Tylenol reduces pain and fever about as well as aspirin, but it has no effect on swelling. Many people who are sensitive to aspirin find it less irritating to their stomachs.

Xylocaine. See *Procaine.*

Amphetamines

Doctors have prescribed amphetamines by trade names, such as Desoxyn and Daprisal. Pharmacists have dispensed them by their generic name, d-amphetamine sulfate. Athletes who have used them call them uppers, greenies, black beauties, yellowjackets, speed, or Vitamin S.

Amphetamines have been among the most used and most abused of modern drugs — not just by athletes but also by housewives, truck drivers, students, and others looking for ways to keep their weight down and their alertness up. Pharmaceutical houses have been manufacturing millions of doses of various amphetamine compounds every year. The Food and Drug Administration has estimated that at least three times as many doses are manufactured in unlicensed, unregulated laboratories and sold illegally. But amateur athletes haven't had to settle for cheap imitations. A physician need not be unethical — just indifferent or ill informed — to prescribe amphetamines to athletes who say they need to lose weight. As for professional athletes, they have needed only to put out their hands.

In his autobiography, *Catch You Later*, Cincinnati Reds catcher Johnny Bench, after confessing his own misuse of amphetamines, declares that all his team's trainers were well stocked with Daprisals and that "nobody thought twice about passing them out." Pitcher Gary Nolan, for instance, would "get a couple of Daps in him and he'd start chirping away, just sitting there in the dugout talking a blue streak. His eyes would get all googly and he wouldn't answer a question, just stay as high as he could be and pitch his head off." Pressed by an interviewer, former Reds slugger Pete Rose also admitted he used amphetamines, in the belief that they would help "mentally," and "when you help yourself mentally, it might help your game."

Mental alertness and weight loss are the benefits sought from amphetamines. But are they the actual benefits? As appetite suppressants, amphetamines work for as long as two weeks; after that, they are ineffective. Old eating patterns, unaltered by new habits and unaffected by amphetamines, then return — and so does the weight that had been lost. If this were the whole story, amphetamines would be just another pointless diet gimmick. But this isn't the whole story. By stimulating the central nervous system, amphetamines make many dieters feel different. Depending on their personality, physiology, and expectations, dieters may enjoy the restless, edgy sensation of energy or find it disconcerting and distracting. They all, however, have trouble sleeping, and gradually their appetites return, unless they take an extra pill — and later, a different pill to help them sleep. This is the common road to amphetamine dependency, and it helps to explain why amphetamines have fallen into total disrepute as an effective and safe aid for losing weight. In fact, a growing number of states are outlawing the prescription of amphetamines for any reason, dieting included.

What most athletes want from amphetamines, however, is not long-term weight loss but the short-term sense of enhanced well-being these drugs provide. And they'll get it, but not without risking problems down the road. When amphetamines were developed in the 1930s, they were believed to help relieve chronic depression. As it turned out, they were only temporarily effective in accomplishing this. Increasing the dosage precipitated different and more acute mental symptoms, such as aggression, hallucinations, anxiety, and paranoia. Then, when the dose was reduced, the final drawback was discovered: amphetamine dependency. Amphetamines have now been superseded by a variety of more effective drugs for treating depression.

Most athletes who use amphetamines are neither chronically depressed nor drug dependent. They simply like the good feeling they get, the feeling that they're playing better, with increased energy and staying power. Unhappily, it's only a feeling. What they are actually getting is a chemical that blunts their awareness of fatigue and pain. In the context of a single event, it might seem advantageous to be able to press on beyond the normal limits of endurance by ignoring the body's warning signals that this joint is overextended, that that muscle is overstressed, that the lungs are overtaxed, that the neural circuits are overloaded — and then to be able to win.

These were the perceived benefits behind one of the major sports scandals of the 1960s: the revelation that most of the bicyclists in the grueling Tour de France were depending on amphetamines to keep them going and, in some cases, to help them win. What put the benefits in perspective was the risk: the scandal broke because a drugged Belgian entrant was so able to ignore his body's warning signals that he collapsed and died of heatstroke.

Amphetamine abuse has led investigators to explore what the drugs can do to improve athletic performance. Surprisingly, they have found that the short-term, mood-elevating effect of amphetamines does not translate into any performance benefit whatsoever. These drugs don't increase endurance because they have no effect on oxygen intake and because they constrict blood vessels, thereby boosting blood pressure and raising heart rate. In the laboratory, amphetamines have a very minor effect on very simple big-muscle movements. Yet, on the playing field, this effect has produced no detectable burst-of-strength or burst-of-speed improvement, perhaps because even the simplest athletic act represents a complex set of muscular and mental reactions.

The ability of amphetamines to mask fatigue and pain short-circuits the most important biofeedback mechanisms. It is in these respects that amphetamines, far from increasing mental alertness, interfere with judgment by denying their users essential information. The risks are greatest when people are exercising and sweating. Thirst is an all-too-easy signal for athletes to ignore. Amphetamines make it a cinch, and also make it possible for them to push past the point at which they are so dehydrated and their internal temperature is so high that they would normally pass out.

If amphetamines cannot improve your game — if, at best, they can only keep you feeling fine while you're falling apart — then why are they so popular? Some professionals think that feeling fine is reason enough. Psychological preparedness matters a lot for big-time athletes in high-pressure situations. They may even have more confidence in pills than in the pregame pep talks that are supposed to psych them up. Even the corniest pep talk, however, lacks the predictable side effects of amphetamines: insomnia, impaired judgment, longer recovery time, increased aggression and hostility.

There are some offensive linebackers who believe that amphetamine-induced paranoia aids them on their search-and-destroy missions. Even they should think twice about amphetamine dependency. It's not the same as addiction, but it's uncomfortably close. It also induces the kinds of crazy behavior that cannot be left on the field or in the locker room.

Steroids

Athletes in power sports, looking for the modern equivalent of a magic potion, feel they have found it in a group of drugs known as androgenic-anabolic steroids. Steroids have been on the sports scene since the 1950s. By the 1964 Olympics in Tokyo, their use was widespread. Four years later, it was being said that 80 percent of Olympic athletes in strength events were on them. At the 1972 Olympics in Munich, two-thirds of the athletes in sprinting, jumping, throwing, and strength events privately admitted having used steroids during their training.

That steroids have since been banned in international competitions hasn't stopped athletes and their trainers from experimenting with them. They must, they say, to avoid being at a competitive disadvantage. Many observers, for example, claim that steroids account for the Soviet domination of weightlifting. The Soviet bloc has indeed institutionalized steroid use, and their experience with these drugs has also made them better able to avoid detection. In this, however, they haven't been entirely successful, nor has the United States. Several of their women athletes have lost European titles for using steroids. And, in the summer of 1981, American discus thrower Ben Plucknett became the first athlete to forfeit a world record for failing a steroid test.

Before the fear of detection becomes an effective deterrent to steroid use, testing will have to become more accurate and more evenly applied than it is at present. This will require a considerable investment of time and money. Even then, it will have no impact on the wide — and legal — use of steroids by football players, wrestlers, and boxers, and their almost universal use by competitive bodybuilders. Like their track and field counterparts, these athletes and their trainers harbor an almost unshakable belief that steroids make it possible to train harder, recover faster, and build more muscle and bulk. It may come as a surprise, then, for you to learn that there is *no consistent or conclusive evidence that steroids work*. Can all those incredible hulks be wrong? The best answer is somewhere between perhaps and probably.

Steroid use, in and out of sports, has been the subject of intense medical scrutiny for several decades now. The drugs were originally developed to treat arthritis, anemia, and various bone and skin disorders. They resemble male hormones both chemically and functionally (this is what *androgenic* means). Therefore, in people with hormone deficiencies, they promote growth, accelerate bone maturation, and cause weight gain (this tissue-building effect is what *anabolic* means). The androgenic effect promotes "virilization," the development of such secondary male growth characteristics as facial hair. Researchers have been trying to increase the anabolic potential and reduce the androgenic potential of steroids. That they have not been particularly successful and that steroids have numerous side effects explain why physicians don't view them as important additions to their pharmacological arsenal. Still, anything that builds tissue and adds weight is bound to attract the attention of athletes and their coaches. And, because the sale of anabolic steroids is not regulated by law, coaches can and do "prescribe" them for promising athletes who are willing to take them to improve their performance. But do they work?

"Anabolic steroids in healthy, young athletes are not fully understood. Studies show conflicting results of increase in strength and
improvement in performance." This is one conclusion of an International Federation of Sports and Medicine symposium on steroids. Recently, the American College of Sports Medicine, having
surveyed all the available evidence, came to its conclusions about
these drugs: First, medically approved doses of steroids don't improve strength, endurance, muscle mass, or body weight. Second,
the evidence that larger doses — the kind that most athletes take
but that no doctor could ethically prescribe — work better is in-
consistent and inconclusive. Third, contrary to a common belief
among athletes, high-protein diets don't make steroids work more
effectively than regular diets.

These findings indicate that steroids work a lot less effectively
than the athletes who use them swear they do. Tom Ecker, the
coach of the Swedish Olympic team in 1966, reporting on steroid
use by European and American athletes, has insisted: "The results
in increased strength and bulk — not endurance — are fantastic.
Neil Steinauer, for example, was rated as the second-best shotput-
ter in the world the year after he started taking steroids, but the
year before he wasn't even in the top fifty *U.S.* shotputters!" In
1981, after setting his world record in the discus but before forfeit-
ing it, Ben Plucknett explained his remarkable improvement in the
preceding year this way: "It's new confidence in my throwing and
training. My whole training routine is different. I don't want to go
into details, but every year I add things and take out things." Understandably, you might conclude that the "detail" he had added
to his training was steroids and that the steroids worked. However,
there are more plausible explanations.

The first is a placebo effect. Athletes who believe in and take
steroids credit the gains they make to steroids. Yet, as the International Federation's report points out, "most users of steroids feel
that the beneficial effects in strength occur only when accompanied
by heavy workouts — usually weight training." Credit should
probably go to the heavy weight training, which itself builds
strength, rather than to the steroids — which do not work out if
you don't. If steroids do work, they may function indirectly by
masking fatigue, thus allowing their users to work harder. As athletes on amphetamines have found, this is a double-edged sword —
one that invites overtraining and injury.

What about the stories of remarkable weight gain from taking steroids? Steroids are known to promote water retention, and they may also stimulate appetite. They may even promote weight gain by *reducing* the overall activity level. If they do, they do so by making their users feel bad — proof enough for some athletes that the steroids are "working" — making them moody, and interfering with their sleep patterns. Even though these athletes may still be able to get it up for their training sessions, they may be less active and energetic overall — an easy way to gain weight, with or without steroids.

Other factors may or may not affect steroid effectiveness: for example, the specific drug taken (there are many), the dosage (at best, a wild guess), the form (pill or injection), and individual sensitivity to the drug. Even if all these factors work in your favor, don't expect too much. Steroids cannot provide what nature has not. Many great athletes have overcome physical limitations, but only with determination and effort.

It may still seem hard to square the evidence before your eyes with the medical evidence that steroids have little, if any, effect. Consider all the world records that have been broken in the past twenty-five years, or compare competitive bodybuilders then and now. How is it possible that steroids don't work? Here's how: The single most dramatic improvement in sports in the past twenty-five years has been in training techniques. Training — not steroids — is the reason why a twelve-year-old girl can swim faster than Johnny Weissmuller ever did, and the main reason why Arnold Schwarzenegger makes Steve Reeves look like a ninety-eight-pound weakling. Major changes in athletic equipment, in the prevention and treatment of sports injuries, and in the understanding of nutrition's role in fueling performance, especially in endurance events, have also contributed. Last, and least, there are drugs. Compared with what athletes want and think they're getting from such drugs, the actual impact of steroids on performance is entirely underwhelming.

In this perspective, steroids would rank with protein supplements and vitamin pills if they didn't have such serious side effects. By altering the body's natural hormone balance, steroids affect virtually every cell in the body, but most notably the liver, kidneys, and cardiovascular and reproductive systems. In 80 percent of regular users, steroids cause detectable liver damage. Other common drawbacks are water retention, low blood sugar, acne, irritability and insomnia, nausea, and diarrhea. Ironically, considering muscle's macho image, prolonged steroid use can also decrease the size, function, and sperm production of the testicles. In fully grown, otherwise healthy, male athletes, most of these effects are thought to be reversible. But the long-term dangers won't be known for ten to twenty years. Nevertheless, medical experience with other forms of hormone manipulation suggest that cancer may be a risk.

Steroids pose an even greater threat to growing athletes, partly because their reproductive systems are still maturing and hardly need the confusion of synthetic hormones. Steroids can also cause the growth plates in the long bones to close prematurely. Many athletes continue to grow throughout their teens, and steroids can cut this growth short.

Steroids are roughest of all on women. The side effects are obvious in many female East German athletes. They look like men, and, in these cases, appearances aren't deceiving. Reacting to the synthetic male hormones in their systems, they do bulk up. In addition, they stop menstruating, their voices deepen, they grow facial hair, and their clitorises enlarge. They are also much more likely to become sterile or to bear defective offspring. Saddest, perhaps, is that much of this damage is irreversible. Why do they take these risks? Young East German women are formidable swimmers, but so are young American women, whose trainers, parents, and physicians are unwilling to pay the price that steroids exact. Unhappily, this is not always the case with American women in other sports. At a time when women are coming into their own in sports, it is discouraging to note that some are willing to take, or can be persuaded to take, drugs that make them more masculine. If the situation were reversed — if, for example, steroids caused male athletes to develop breasts — their use would disappear overnight.

But what if you've got "pecs," not breasts? And what if you're convinced that without steroids you won't win the next Mr. Megabody contest? Can steroids be taken safely? No. Can the risks be reduced? Maybe. But the only way to make the risks associated with the "maybe" acceptable is to get steroids from a doctor — not from a coach and not from a friend. Even then, take a tip from someone at the top. In a recent issue of *Muscle and Fitness*, Ray Mentzer discussed the results of the medically supervised steroid

---

A Steroid ℞ for Young Men

If you do not loom as large as you would like and have considered steroids, you now know their dangers for growing athletes. But what if an overeager coach, buddy, or parent — well intentioned but dangerously misinformed — is pushing you to take steroids? If you think that you have to play ball with them in order to play ball at all, let them give you the pills — then throw them away. Work out with weights and, following the Eat-to-Win guidelines, eat as much as you comfortably can six to eight times a day. You are guaranteed to bulk up, and no one except you and your body will ever be the wiser.

---

program he followed before winning the Mr. America contest. Did the drugs work? "1 was perhaps 1–2 percent bigger and 1–2 percent harder looking." But steroids were no substitute for "PHD" — persistence, hard work, and dedication. As he also made clear: "The mental intensity that drives a person through his workouts cannot be produced by steroids. And a person who believes these drugs are the answer has no faith in his abilities. Thus steroids are a symbol of a lack of self-confidence."

* * *

A hardy mythology has grown up about the magical powers of drugs. For every test that shows they don't work, there are plenty of athletes who swear they do. Belief is a potent energizer. This is why we need such things as double-blind studies, which let us eliminate the belief factor and uncover the facts. Even facts won't convince some enthusiasts, of course. They're sure that the authorities are holding out, trying to protect them, afraid that if they find out how good drugs actually are, they'll be beating down the pharmacy doors. Maybe even these athletes will believe the results from studies of the effects of drugs on another group of sports performers: thoroughbred race horses.

Drugging horses is an even bigger taboo than drugging athletes. In France, however, a group of horse racers decided to find out the facts. For over five years, they ran horses in every conceivable condition: with and without drugs, fresh and fatigued, warmed up

155

and cold. As it turned out, there was no drug that would improve a horse's performance. Drugs would mask fatigue, enabling horses to run beyond safe limits. But even then, they didn't run better.

We're left with a paradox. Because of the myth that drugs make athletes and race horses perform better, their use has been prohibited. Yet the overwhelming evidence is that *drugs are not ergogenic.*

PART THREE

The Training Table

12

How to Eat to Win

All of us deep down inside have some feelings about our own self-image and what we want it to be. In these intimate aspects of life, we have to answer to ourselves. So make up your mind to begin your program now and stay with it.

The President's Council
on Physical Fitness and Sports

Life is not worth living without Twinkies.

HAL HIGDON
Editor-at-large, *Runner's World*

HAVE YOU EVER HAD a bad sports habit that you had to break? A faulty grip, or poor pacing, or a tendency to duck your head? Remember how difficult it was to correct your technique? Initially, the change felt all wrong, even though you knew it was right. With practice, everything fell into place, and now you can't imagine doing it any way but the right way.

The same thing will happen when you switch to an Eat-to-Win diet. It's both unrealistic and unfair to suggest that the change will be easy. Force of habit makes any change, however attractive in theory, seem difficult and unrewarding in practice — until it all falls together. Therefore the first thing to ask yourself is, Do I really want to change the way I eat? Because there are perfectly valid reasons *not* to.

Only in the strictest, scientific sense is food just fuel and eating merely tanking up. Eating is a private joy, and dining is one of humankind's most civilized social rituals. Our reasons for finding eating pleasurable go beyond the satisfaction of hunger. These reasons have their roots in cultural practices that have existed for centuries, family customs that are generations old, and personal preferences that date back to infancy, when food was the first tangible expression of our parents' love and care. As a result, eating has symbolic meanings, psychological benefits, and emotional satisfactions that are just as life enhancing as those that come from eating the way we "should."

So powerful are these non-nutritional factors that it is entirely possible for the way you eat to seem life enhancing — in the sense that it makes you feel good — yet to be life threatening — in the sense that it increases your chances of developing heart disease. With the Eat-to-Win plan, the way you eat will make you feel good and will be good for you at the same time. But it won't necessarily seem that way at first. Any time you make a change, what you give up will initially be a lot more apparent than what you gain — unless you have a positive motivation for change.

When coaches remind their players that they might not win even with all the motivation in the world but they cannot win without it, they are voicing one of the great truisms of competition. This home truth holds for diet and nutrition as well. You will not break bad nutritional habits without proper motivation. Do you feel an uneasiness about your eating patterns? Do you feel a little guilty because you aren't taking better care of yourself? If you do, stay the way you are. Fear and guilt are the least effective motives for change. As any psychologist will say, they invariably lead to resentment, resistance, rebellion — and no change. If "cookie therapy" works for you, stay with it. Giving it up because you know you "should" will make the Eat-to-Win diet a joyless — and ultimately unsuccessful — sacrifice.

The only way you will discover that the Eat-to-Win plan is at least as satisfying as the way you now eat is to approach it with a positive motivation, not a punitive one. Your motive may be pragmatic: you need more energy or less weight to get where you want to go in your sport. It may be emotional: you deserve the best. Or it may be philosophical: you want your behavior to be in harmony with your beliefs. Whatever your motive, a positive attitude is essential in helping you over the transitional rough spots.

Once you've decided to change your diet, you need a plan. Habits are hard to break, and the habits formed earliest are the hardest. Unfortunately, you've been in training since infancy to prefer foods that are loaded with added fat, sugar, and salt. These most powerful flavor enhancers have numbed your taste buds. It's the foods themselves, of course, that have the flavor to begin with. But you've lost the ability to appreciate the subtleties of simpler, less processed foods. You *can* reeducate your taste buds to prefer foods that are lighter, less salty, and less sweet. However, during the transition period — until your taste becomes more finely tuned — food will seem to have lost some of its taste appeal. At this point, there is one thing that may be essential to keep you going: proof.

The Three-Day Demonstration Diet

If you are game for an experiment in the laboratory you know best — your own body — then, in only three days, you can prove to yourself that you can liberate your taste buds. You can do so by testing the Eat-to-Win Intensive Training plan. It's a nutritionally superior plan with several practical limitations. Because it almost totally restricts the use of added fat, sugar, and salt, the diet is quite different from the way you now eat and also from the Eat-to-Win Basic Training plan.

The intensive-training is one to be followed occasionally: when you want to *over*correct after overindulging, when you want to lose weight without sacrificing energy, when low body weight or low body fat is vitally important in your sport, or when you want to bring yourself to the peak of nutritional fitness. This is another one of those occasions. Three days on the Intensive Training plan can rescue your taste buds from oblivion. You will learn how easy it is to live all the time with a lot less fat, sugar, and salt — because you like it that way.

On the first day, your food will taste different. In fact, it will taste like cardboard. Well, perhaps not that good. By the second day, you will detect gradations in flavor that you never noticed before. Not all cardboard tastes the same. By the third day, your food will begin tasting like food. Not great food, but acceptable. Of course, you wouldn't want to eat this way all the time (and you won't have to).

The Eat-to-Win Requirements

Basic Training

1. You determine how much to eat on the basis of your weight goal.

2. Eat as often as you want, but at least three times a day.

3. Each meal's main component is a high-carbohydrate food (bread, pasta, potatoes, rice, cereal) and a smaller serving of a high-protein food (meat, fish, eggs, beans, nuts, dairy products). Aim for variety.

4. Eat as many vegetables as you want, but at least two different ones a day. Aim for variety.

5. Eat as much fruit as you want, but at least one citrus fruit and one noncitrus fruit a day. Aim for variety. In summer, or when sweating heavily, add an extra fruit.

6. As a general rule, avoid all foods with added fat, sugar, and salt.

7. Treat yourself to one high-fat and one high-sugar food a day if you have no weight problem.

8. Limit liquids with calories except skim milk, low-fat buttermilk, and vegetable and 100 percent fruit juices; alcohol is okay in moderation.

Intensive Training

1–5. Same as requirements 1–5 for basic training.

6. To reduce your fat intake, eat meat once a day or less, and use only low-fat milk and dairy products, dips, dressings, and sauces. Avoid all processed, convenience, and fast foods.

7. To reduce your sugar intake, add no sugar in any form to your food. (Also restrict saccharin to one item — coffee, for example.)

8. Drink no liquids with calories (including alcoholic beverages) except skim milk, low-fat buttermilk, and vegetable and fruit drinks that you make from fresh fruits and vegetables.

9. Eat only unsalted cereals and crackers.

10. Allow yourself one treat a day, preferably one that isn't high in sugar.

On the fourth day, when you return to your regular eating habits, whole milk will taste like heavy cream. High-sugar drinks and desserts will be too sweet and snack foods too salty. Your three-day experiment will have demonstrated that your taste buds are far more trainable than you realized. You can, of course, reaccustom them to high-fat, high-sugar, high-salt foods all over again. But now you have a way to correct those problems whenever you think they're getting out of hand.

The Intensive Training diet is a crashless crash diet, an extreme intervention but a healthful and helpful one. It will work for anyone but it isn't an answer for everyone. It will suit you if you're a skeptic with a show-me attitude, or if you're the kind of enthusiast who plunges rather than eases into icy pools, rips rather than peels off Band-Aids, and shouts "Let's put on a show" before you know if anyone has a barn. In addition, following the diet for three days can be a benign form of penance for the well-intentioned but guilt-ridden who have temporarily strayed from the nutritional straight and narrow.

Yet there is one thing the Intensive Training diet is not. Except for extremists, it isn't a substitute for the everyday eating patterns that are essential to the Eat-to-Win plan. It can serve as an introduction to those patterns, but the real training challenge remains: making the transition from conscious choices to automatic behavior, reaching the point where everything suddenly falls into place and you can't imagine eating any other way. This takes practice — the same kind of training effort you put into your sport. The only differences are that you'll be doing the training in the supermarket, in the kitchen, and at the training table, whether it's at home or on the road.

Theoretical Goals and Practical Considerations

The first two parts of this book have presented the case for removing as much fat, sugar, and salt from your diet and adding as much fruit, vegetable, and grain to it as you reasonably can. The following basic tips, which you can use anywhere and anytime, provide a strategy that will help you achieve this goal.

1. *Get back to basics.* Fresh and minimally processed foods offer

maximum nutrients with minimal added fat, sugar, and salt. Remember that every processing step decreases nutrients and almost invariably adds calories. If you like fruit drinks, which are high in added sugar, try fruit juices or, better yet, the fruits themselves. If you like to snack on fruit-flavored yogurt, which gets almost half its calories from sugar, try plain, low-fat yogurt with a piece of fresh fruit.

2. *Learn to visualize fat and sugar.* You probably know that ice cream is mostly fat and sugar, that shortening is all fat, and that avocados and nuts are high in fat. But what do you see when you look at meat? Protein? You should also see half-fat, because, on the average, this is what meat is. And when you pick up a snack bar — even those that are billed "all-natural" — you should see fat and sugar, because these are their main ingredients. To help you visualize the fat and sugar in food, here are some guidelines. (Foods that are high in added salt are denoted by italics.)

LITTLE OR NO FAT: plain fruits and vegetables; basic grains and grain products (bread, rice, pasta); beans; skim and low-fat milk; low-fat dairy products (cottage cheese, yogurt, buttermilk); *canned broths*

MODERATE FAT: *frozen vegetables in sauces; canned, non-creamed soups and sauces; canned pasta and pork-and-beans,* canned, water-packed chicken, turkey, and seafood (including tuna)

HALF FAT: most meats; *fast foods;* fried foods; *most frozen convenience foods; creamed soups and sauces; potato chips, corn chips, pretzels, and so forth*

HIGH FAT: cheeses; cream; *processed meats;* eggs; nuts; peanut butter

ALL (OR VIRTUALLY ALL) FAT: vegetable oils; butter; margarine; lard, shortenings; mayonnaise; *salad dressings*

ALL (OR VIRTUALLY ALL) SUGAR: soft drinks, fruit drinks; syrups; gelatin desserts; hard candies; refined sugars; honey; jams, jellies, and so forth

MOSTLY FAT AND SUGAR: candies, desserts (cakes, frostings, pies, cookies, ice cream, ice milk, frozen yogurt); instant breakfasts; granola; snack and "energy" bars; reconstituted and liquid meals; milk shakes

The better you become at looking at a food and visualizing it in terms of added fat, sugar, and salt, the easier it will be to make informed choices, which will eventually become automatic.

3. *Read labels.* By law, manufacturers have to specify on their labels what is in the foods they produce. The ingredients are supposed to be listed in order of decreasing weight. Labeling laws aren't perfect — for example, labels don't specify how much salt has been added — but they do give us a fighting chance.

We'd expect a Ring-Ding to contain corn syrup, shortening, sugar, whey, and enriched flour. But what about Carnation's Breakfast Bar, the one that supposedly makes milk a nutritious meal? Its three main ingredients are sugar, malted milk, and oil. Nature Valley Granola Clusters are built a bit differently. They contain rolled oats, brown sugar, coconut oil, almond pieces, honey, sugar, and so forth, but the message is the same: fat and sugar. (Notice how manufacturers like to divide the sugars, perhaps in an attempt to conquer consumers.) Carnation Instant Breakfast lists among its ingredients nonfat dry milk, sugar, sweet dairy whey, corn-syrup solids, calcium caseinate, and lactose. Not every consumer is going to know that corn syrup and lactose are sugars, although they might suspect that the whey isn't sweet without reason.

You may be enlightened by this "important nutritional fact" on packages of Ruffles potato chips: a one-ounce serving (bet you can't eat just one ounce) has no more calories than a glass of milk. Imagine that. Before you toss out the milk to make room for the Ruffles, remember what else the package tells you, because it's required to: Ruffles contains potatoes, fat, and salt, and one ounce of these chips has 150 calories and 10 grams of fat. A more helpful way of putting it, which may be why they don't, is that an ounce of Ruffles is 60 percent fat (1 gram of fat has 9 calories, so 90 of those 150 calories — 60 percent — are fat). What you do not get from Ruffles that you do get from milk is protein, calcium, and vitamins A and D.

Labeling gives the kind of information that can help you make choices. For example, if a Thomas' English Muffin has 130 calories and 1 gram of fat, should you opt for it rather than a Thomas' Toast-r-Cake with 110 calories and 4 grams of fat? It depends. Would you slather the first with butter but eat the second as is? The best choice, however, is the muffin, spread with a little low-fat cottage cheese. Similarly, should you switch to diet margarine and diet mayonnaise? That depends on whether you like the taste of the diet products and are more concerned with calories than cost. Then diet margarine, which gets all its calories from fat but is fluffed up with added water, is the better choice. But a still better choice is a spread that is low in fat, such as cottage cheese or yogurt.

4. *Explore alternatives.* One of the advantages of the variety of foods on grocery shelves is that there is almost always something with less fat and sugar that you can learn to enjoy. Consider soft drinks, for example. You know they're just flavored sugar water. You could switch to sugar-free versions, but maybe you don't want the saccharin or can't take the taste. One alternative is to explore the chic world of bottled waters. Another is to use ordinary seltzer or all-fruit juices. A third is to dilute fruit juices with seltzer or water. The result is a lightly flavored drink that will, at first, taste watery. Later, it will seem far more refreshing than the cloyingly sweet soft drinks you used to like.

5. *Accept no substitutes.* A lot of foods are trying to be what they aren't, which is why they're such failures. We tolerate sugar-free soft drinks, for example, but do we really like them? Their sweetness isn't true, substantial, or satisfying. They are among the many foods that can be classified as alternatives-that-aren't: eggless eggs, nondairy creamers (which are mostly fat and sugar), meatless meats, diet margarines, cheeseless cheeses (all very high in fat), diet cream cheese, and so forth. Some such foods are chemical concoctions, with nothing to offer but calories. Others represent sincere efforts to offer reasonably nutritious alternatives. Yet they are all based on a common premise: that we are helpless to control our diets, and that the only way we might be able to change is with foods that fake it. Let's not kid ourselves. The only way the vegetables, beans, and grains in a veggie-burger are going to taste like hamburger is if we feed them to a cow, and eat the cow.

When you make a substitution, approach it as a new food and you won't be disappointed. Grapefruit juice cut with seltzer is a tart and tangy thirst-quencher — and just as addictive as Bubble-Up or Fresca. Just don't palm it off as a soft drink. It's different.

6. *Make adjustments.* There's a foolproof way to cut the amount of fat, sugar, and salt in foods that have them in abundance: eat smaller portions. We're used to having meat be the largest serving on our plate. It should be the smallest. We're also used to having

the potato, rice, or pasta be the smallest. It should be the largest. Vegetables too should loom larger than the meat. Unlike grains and beans, they are so low in calories you can also eat them in abundance in side dishes or salads. Remember too that the most traditional-looking meal may get most of its fat from dressings, gravies, and table margarine or butter. Finding acceptable substitutes for these and for sweet, creamy desserts can have more of a nutritional impact than adjusting the meal itself.

7. *Deny yourself nothing.* The Eat-to-Win plan does not require you to enter a nutritional nunnery. Self-denial is an entirely overrated virtue that makes people unbearable or frustrated. Sacrifices are for saints; cheating is for sinners. The Eat-to-Win plan is for regular people, and there is no food that it forbids. Is life not worth living without Twinkies? Do you need a regular frankfurter fix? Make a list of the foods you would miss if you were to become a nutritional purist. Allow yourself one of these treats every day. Or accumulate credits and have a pig-out. When a treat is truly a treat, it requires no justification and entails no guilt. It is simply an inconsequential element in an overall eating pattern.

8. *Distinguish treats from habits.* If the list you just made is a long one, keep in mind that when a treat becomes habitual, it's no longer a treat — it's a habit. Replacing old habits with nutritionally superior new ones is the only way to eat to win successfully. You might find that foods that seem essential now aren't so important once you've discovered equally enjoyable but more nutritious new ones.

9. *Distinguish real from fake convenience.* There are a lot of so-called convenience foods that really aren't. For example, preparing a TV dinner requires heating the oven, peeling back or poking through the aluminum wrapper, popping the tray into the oven, and waiting thirty to forty minutes — all this for what is, at best, a mediocre meal with excessive fat and salt. You can gratify your hunger faster with a plate of pasta and a salad, and it will taste better and be more nutritious. But who says you have to cook? If you are really in a hurry, you can make a sandwich or a salad in the time it would take to heat the oven.

10. *Don't play the numbers racket.* You can eliminate a lot of fat, sugar, and salt from your diet yet fall numerically short of the Eat-to-Win goals. Don't worry. You're still a winner, because you've

managed the toughest trick of all: you've actually changed your eating patterns.

11. *Concentrate on your goal.* Don't get so caught up in details that you forget what really matters: your basic eating patterns and ways to improve them. You need to make conscious choices now, but you will eat to win only if they become automatic. When this happens — and it will — you won't be thinking about how to eat to win. You'll be doing it.

13

Shopping to Win

Why can't the food industry protect us from nutritional illusion? Theoretically, it could. But the
industrial reality is that, while production methods are controlled by technologists of great so-
phistication, the businesses are guided by market-
ers. Their training is in the economics of producing
and selling. Their information about nutrition is
minimal. Their primary interest lies in what will
sell, and this is determined by what the public
wants. Their foremost research effort is to determine public wishes and to meet them.

RONALD M. DEUTSCH
Realities of Nutrition

IF AN EATING PLAN is to have universal value, then the foods
it calls for must be universally available. To eat to win, you don't
have to live down the street from a truck farm or around the corner
from a health-food store. You don't have to bake your own bread
or keep a root cellar. You just need to have access to a typical
American supermarket. It's an incredible place, offering a staggering variety of foods that are good, not so good, and pretty awful,
with the least nutritious invariably the most heavily promoted.

It may be difficult at first to maintain your equilibrium when
confronted with shoppers overloading their carts with food that is
overloaded with fat, sugar, and salt. For almost every simple,
straightforward, unadorned food, there will be a dozen others that
have been manufactured from simpler foods, laced with chemicals,
then flavored and held together with fat, sugar, and salt. But don't

start your shopping expedition with a heavy heart. The simple, unadulterated foods are there — and they are the best and most nutritious buys.

Meats

There are many strategies, but the goal is always the same: to cut your meat intake by one-third, one-half, or even more. It's the primary way to reduce your intake of animal fat, which is as large a component of meat as protein is. Happily, buying less meat will save you a lot of money, and it may not alter your eating patterns as dramatically as you might think.

One choice you can make is to stop regularly buying processed meats. They are especially high in fat and, despite their seemingly lower prices, actually extremely expensive sources of protein compared with meats that are closer to the hoof or beak. Processed meat comes in endless forms: breaded and frozen in the freezer case; stuffed, rolled, chipped, reformed, and presented as sausages, franks, and luncheon meats.

What about switching to lean meats? There is a significant trend in this direction in our national meat consumption. Chicken, turkey, and lean, unmarbled meats have less fat than hamburger, which, in turn, has less fat than beef steaks, roasts, and chops, as well as ham and pork. If limiting yourself to lean meats sounds limiting, remember that trimming all visible fat from high-fat meats can cut the amount of fat per serving by as much as 50 percent.

Still, there's no getting around the facts that we eat an average of almost twice our weight in meat each year and that this amount is too much. Some of the cooking strategies presented in the next chapter will help, but the basic way to cut meat intake is to save money in the meat department.

Seafood

As if you hadn't noticed, fresh seafood can be expensive. It's also high in protein and low in fat, and an excellent replacement for meat. Tuna is by far the most commonly consumed fish in this country. It's relatively inexpensive, precooked, and versatile. Tuna packed in oil has twice the calories of tuna packed in water, so buying the water-packed variety is another easy way to eliminate added fat. Other kinds of canned seafood vary considerably in price. Mackerel, salmon, clams, and sardines are usually cheaper than shrimp and crab but just as nutritious. Check the labels, however, to see whether they're packed in salt water (brine) or oil. Frozen, breaded seafood sticks, fillets, and cakes all contain added fat and salt, and are no substitute for fresh seafood or meat.

Milk and Dairy Products

The dairy case is a place where you can get some of your best buys and also save hundreds of calories a day in animal fat.

Start with milk. No adult needs whole milk. Skim milk has half the calories and none of the fat. It may taste thin at first, but even this difference is unnoticeable when the milk is on cereal or in coffee. If you drink milk by the glass and won't drink skim, try low-fat milk that is only 1 percent fat. As with low-fat yogurt, cottage cheese, and buttermilk, there is virtually no difference in taste but a significant saving in fat.

Some people have to acquire a taste for low-fat milk products. Others find them bland. But they are tremendously useful in making low-fat sauces, dressings, and dips when combined with a dried soup or salad mix or with your own seasonings. Nonfat dry milk is an ideal coffee or tea creamer. If you carry an artificial sweetener with you, you should also be carrying a small jar of nonfat dry milk.

Except for farmer's and cottage cheeses, most cheeses are two-thirds fat. In a low-fat diet, if you have cheese, don't have meat at the same meal. Or limit cheese to the status of a treat. A tablespoon of grated cheese like Parmesan or Romano, however, can add a disproportionate amount of flavor to vegetables and pasta for the 50 calories — 35 from fat — that it contains.

A number of the reduced-fat cheeses on the market are nutritious. Whether they will be useful depends on how they taste to you and how you use them. Kraft Imitation Cream Cheese has most of the taste and half the calories of regular cream cheese. Nevertheless, it gets 70 percent of its calories from fat (compared with 90 percent for real cream cheese). Part-skim-milk ricotta and mozzarella also have less fat than their counterparts made from all whole milk but still rank as high-fat foods. In some American-style reduced-fat cheeses, fat accounts for 35 percent of calories, rather than 50 percent. This is a significant reduction, but the same reduction can be achieved by eating less cheese to begin with.

Compare, for example, the calories and fat in cheese sandwiches made with the following amounts and kinds of cheeses (and without butter, margarine, or mayonnaise):

1. Two slices of regular American cheese — 440 calories, with 180 calories (40 percent) from fat.
2. One slice of regular American cheese — 330 calories, with 100 calories (30 percent) from fat.
3. Two slices of reduced-fat American cheese: 380 calories, with 72 calories (20 percent) from fat.
4. One slice of reduced-fat American cheese: 280 calories, with 45 calories (16 percent) from fat.

This comparison illustrates how simple choice can dramatically reduce the fat intake without dramatically changing the choice of food. A weight-conscious athlete will benefit from the last sandwich in the list. And so will a hungry athlete — simply by eating two.

Eggs

Eggs are extremely nutritious. They are also the main source of cholesterol in the average diet. Whether you are concerned about dietary cholesterol or not, you should still approach eggs with some reserve, for they're two-thirds fat. Use them where you appreciate them the most, and try to avoid the additional calories from fat that you would get if you fried them.

Oils and Other Fats

Although there's a lot of hidden fat in many processed foods, we eat a fair amount of butter, margarine, mayonnaise, shortening, and vegetable oil. All of these get 90–100 percent of their calories from fat, which we get by adding them to sauces and dressings, spreading them on bread, or cooking with them. In every instance, there are options.

You can poach, steam, or bake most foods as easily as you can fry them. You can buy reduced-fat salad dressings. Even better, by combining yogurt, buttermilk, or tomato juice with fresh or dried herbs or with a package of dried salad seasonings, you can make a salad dressing that contains little or no fat.

Using margarine or butter as a table spread is an easy way to add a lot of unwanted fat to your diet. Whipped versions, which have been fluffed up with air, and "diet" margarines, which have been extended with water, never seem to cost less. And you may simply find yourself using more. Remember, as with imitation mayonnaise, these things still get 90 percent of their calories or more from fat.

An easier approach is to save butter and mayonnaise for times when you really want and appreciate their flavors. At other times, try something else — an herb spread made with farmer's or cottage cheese, for example.

Breads

By now, you should know why you were mistaken if you have ever settled for a simple steak and salad, and passed up the bread because you were watching your calories. As with pasta, potatoes, and rice, the problem isn't the bread, but what we put on it. Bread itself fully merits its staff-of-life status. It's high in the complex carbohydrates we need for energy, and it's a useful source of protein, some vitamins, and — if it's been made from whole grains — fiber too.

Bread is also low in fat. Usually, less than 15 percent of its calories are from fat. English muffins are around 7 percent; pita (Middle Eastern bread, also known as pouch bread or sandwich pockets) is a bit lower. Pita is particularly handy because the cavity that is created during baking can be stuffed with chopped vegetables, cottage cheese, and other foods that would fall out of a regular sandwich.

Breads right out of the oven are incomparable. Whole-grain

breads have more flavor, texture, and fiber than white bread. For some people, fluffy white bread epitomizes everything that is wrong with the way we eat. But if you prefer it, take comfort in the fact that the main thing you are missing is fiber. So buy the brand you enjoy eating. Even better, try a variety. If you're buying a bread with added fiber, however, check the label to make sure the fiber isn't cellulose derived from wood pulp. It's safe, but it's not the form of fiber you need. Your goal is to eat more grain, not trees.

Rice and Potatoes

Like bread and pasta, rice and potatoes are important for their carbohydrates, B vitamins, and several minerals. (Potatoes are the only staple that contain some vitamin C.) Similarly, they also contain modest amounts of protein. This protein is made more usable when eaten — as it almost always is — with a complementary vegetable or with meat, eggs, fish, or dairy foods. Like all staples, rice and potatoes don't deserve their reputation as fattening foods. Once again, the high-fat things we put on them are the real culprits.

Brown rice is more flavorful and slightly more nutritious than enriched white rice. A quicker-cooking brown rice has been developed. But despite what the ads imply, even the slowest-cooking rice — brown or white — is as easy to make as boiling water. Those boil-in-the-bag rices are simpler still, but have added fat and salt, and inflated prices.

The potato is America's favorite mealtime filler. Potatoes in their skins are also more nutritious than other staple foods, with the exception of beans. Peeling potatoes closes this gap. Frozen fried potatoes are less nutritious and twice as caloric. Instant mashed potatoes are lower in vitamins than regular potatoes, but you might find them useful as a fast, cheap side dish.

Pasta

Pasta can be the centerpiece of any Eat-to-Win meal. It's high in carbohydrates, and it has some useful protein and practically no fat. For some reason, whole-wheat pasta is two to three times more expensive than regular, enriched pasta. And high-protein pasta isn't worth the money either. Buy enriched pasta. Buy first for taste, then for price. Egg noodles have a little more fat, but the real problem is not the fat in pasta and noodles but the fat in the sauce. Low-calorie commercial sauces are available, but it's easy enough to make your own. Using a little meat in the sauce or sprinkling the pasta with a tablespoon of Parmesan or Romano cheese makes the protein more usable and adds a manageable amount of fat.

Pasta's virtues are lost in the kind of Italian cooking that features lots of cheese, oil, and/or sausage. Low-fat versions of these dishes are usually disasters. So have them once in a while, and then go all the way.

Beans

Americans tend to see beans only in terms of baked beans and chili. But there are many different kinds of dried and canned beans. All of them are undervalued and inexpensive sources of protein and carbohydrates, as well as B vitamins, iron, phosphorus, and magnesium. In fact, calorie for calorie, they are about twice as nutritious as other staples.

Dried beans need only to be soaked and boiled. Every package has a recipe for a hearty soup that's a main meal. Canned beans are somewhat lower in nutrients and considerably higher in salt. But they are precooked and can be added to other dishes, such as salads, without any further preparation. Canned pork-and-beans are about 15 percent fat and also contain some sugar. But they're still nutritious enough to be a useful convenience food. The bean's reputation as the musical fruit is exaggerated. Soaking dried beans in water overnight and discarding the water lessens the problem.

Chips, Crackers, and Similar Snack Foods

Most chips, crackers, pretzels, and similar snack items are fried or baked with a lot of fat and salt. Potato chips, cheese puffs, and tortilla chips, for example, are between 50 percent and 60 percent fat. Because of the way such snacks have been processed, they offer few nutrients other than calories. There are options, however. Scandinavian-style flatbreads, crispbreads, and wafers, matzo crackers, and kosher pretzels are made without shortening. Some are also available without salt. They may taste flat all by themselves, but with a flavorful low-fat dip, they add the crunch, body, and loading platform that are any chip's major contributions to a dip.

Nuts and Peanuts

Nuts and peanuts are good sources of protein and carbohydrates, but they are also high in fat. This limits their usefulness, especially if you are watching your weight. Soy nuts, which are beginning to make an appearance, are lower in oil and different in taste. Both are available in unsalted versions.

Peanut butter is an all-American classic. Combining it with bread makes almost all of its protein usable. You can make a little bit go further by spreading it on warm toast.

Peanuts are also one of the main ingredients in trail mix and "ambrosia." Read the labels carefully, however. A lot of brands are loaded with sugar, which makes a useful but already high-calorie snack even higher in calories. You can save money by making your own trail mix from peanuts, nuts, raisins, and other chopped, dry fruit; add a low-sugar, bite-size cereal if you like.

Cereals

Since breakfast is an ideal and easy opportunity to have a high-energy but fat-free meal, breakfast cereals are an important part of an Eat-to-Win regimen. The range is rather awesome, the choices rather few. Too much sugar is added to many cereals. Granolas and granola-type cereals also have added fat. (And forget about those instant-breakfast mixes and bars. They get two-thirds of their calories from fat and sugar.)

Among the ready-to-eat cereals that *Consumer Reports* has judged best in nutritional quality are Nabisco Shredded Wheat, Post Grape-Nuts, Cheerios, Kellogg's All-Bran, Familia (an expensive import, with one variety having no added sugar), Kretschmer Sun Country

Granola (but with twice the calories of the others per serving), and Quaker Life. Also on the list were several cereals with more than 25 percent sugar: Kellogg's Cracklin' Bran (30 percent) and Frosted Mini-Wheats (26 percent), Honey-Nut Cheerios (33 percent), and Lucky Charms (41 percent).

Among hot cereals, the following were rated best in nutritional quality: Instant Cream of Wheat, Instant Quaker Oatmeal (regular flavor), Quaker Instant Grits, Maypo 30-second Oatmeal (artificial maple flavor), Mix 'n Eat Cream of Wheat (regular flavor), and Quick Cream of Wheat. Two other hot cereals, both high in sugar, made the list: Instant Quaker Oatmeal (artificial maple and brown-sugar flavors; 31 percent), and Mix 'n Eat Cream of Wheat (artificial maple and brown-sugar flavors; 29 percent).

Kellogg's has also introduced four Nutri-Grain whole-grain cereals that are low in sugar. Like other whole-grain cereals, they are good sources of fiber. But are they your best buys? One of the most interesting results of the study is how difficult it is to judge a cereal by its contents. High-sugar cereals made the top category. And such highly fortified brands as Product 19, Total, and Most were in the lowest-ranked group. This is an object lesson in how processing affects nutritional value, and how all the fortification in the world won't guarantee that those vitamins and minerals will actually be absorbed and used.

Vegetables

Americans are hardly having a love affair with vegetables, the consumption of which has risen only 5 percent over the past decade. Confronting a carrot will hardly be the biggest challenge in your life. Yet, unless you can find merit in what many disdain as rabbit food, you'll lose invaluable and low-calorie sources of vitamins, minerals, and fiber.

If you aren't in the habit of shopping for vegetables, consider them alternate salad fixings. As tasty as lettuce is, no lettuce has the nutritional value of broccoli, cauliflower, green peppers, squashes, tomatoes, and carrots. All of these vegetables, along with onions, sprouts, mushrooms, and radishes, are delicious raw. With the exceptions of onions and radishes, all have far subtler flavors when eaten raw.

When buying vegetables, look for firm ones without breaks, bruises, or off-colors. Locally grown, seasonal produce will have more nutrients than any other, but if you don't like the way fresh produce looks on a particular shopping day, don't hesitate to buy frozen. Even though frozen vegetables lose some nutrients during processing, they're better for you than limp carrots and tired broccoli.

The main reason to avoid boil-in-a-bag and canned vegetables is that they contain added fat, salt, or both. For an inflated price, you can buy dietetic-pack canned vegetables, which have no added salt. Salt is added to vegetable juices, and they have fewer nutrients. But they are low in calories, and they can be convenient bases for low-fat sauces and dressings.

Fruits and Juices

Fruit enjoys a better reputation than vegetables, yet the consumption of fresh fruits hasn't risen much in the past decade. Fruits are ideal snacks and desserts, as well as sources of numerous vitamins, minerals, and fiber.

Buy fresh fruits in season, and go for variety. Often overlooked alternatives are dried fruits: raisins, apricots, peaches, prunes, dates, and figs. They retain almost all their nutrients during the drying process, and, because the water has been removed, they can be stored indefinitely. Dried fruits may seem expensive until you consider the amount you're actually getting. Their main drawback is that it is very easy to eat a lot of them without thinking about all the calories you're getting.

Fruit juices have been processed. So they don't have all the nutrients of fresh and dried fruits, and they completely lack fiber. But they're still good foods. Orange juice is the most popular, and probably the simplest way to get our daily allotment of vitamin C. Juice from a can, bottle, or carton contains fewer nutrients than juice from frozen concentrate. Fruit *drinks* — which are mostly sugar and as little as 10 percent juice — should be avoided. Don't fall for the vitamin-C enriched pitch. Juices are often enriched too, but they don't contain added sugar.

Canned fruits are now available packed in fruit juices rather than sugar syrup. They're not as nutritious as fresh fruits, but at least they're no higher in calories. And they can add a welcome note of variety to your diet.

Seasonings and Condiments

Every supermarket has an ample selection of seasonings: herbs, spices, flavor extracts, and sauces. Some of these items have no calories and no salt. Others contain fat, sugar, and salt. In determining which to use, the question is, How do you intend to use them? For example, by weight, ketchup has as much sugar as a chocolate bar, but do you eat it like candy? Soy sauce, hot sauce, Worcestershire sauce, and A-1 Sauce have salt and/or sugar. The salt is of more concern. Although alternatives to most processed foods have been mentioned, dried soups and salad-dressing mixes, canned broths, no-fat crackers, and similar high-salt foods are acceptable because of their flexibility and convenience. (Remember, you get some salt from foods that don't taste at all salty — cottage cheese and bread, for example.)

As mentioned earlier, restricting your use of salt will help reactivate your taste buds and teach them to appreciate the lighter flavors of the fresh and lightly processed foods you will be using.

The seasonings that contain a considerable amount of salt are seasoned salts, meat tenderizers, ketchup, prepared mustards and horseradish, soy sauce, dried salad-dressing and soup mixes, chili sauces and hot sauces, bouillon cubes, pickles, relishes, capers, and olives. (Monosodium glutamate — MSG, which is what Accent is — should also be avoided if you are cutting your intake of sodium chloride — salt.) The ones with no salt are onions, garlic, pepper and other spices (such as chili powder, dry mustard, and ginger), all herbs (dried and fresh), vinegar, lemons, and limes.

Beverages

If you think in terms of *no added sugar* and *low in fat,* you won't go far wrong with what you drink. This attitude eliminates soft drinks, fruit drinks and mixes, whole milk, and liquid-diet meals. It leaves fruit juices, vegetable juices, skim and low-fat milk and buttermilk, and bottled waters. Vegetable juices and bottled waters usually contain added or naturally occurring salt. This is a reason to favor seltzer, which is simply carbonated water. Seltzer is useful for extending and adding variety to juices, white wines, and sangria. Of course, there's always tap water. The taste varies from region to region, but tap water is indisputably the least expensive liquid you can drink.

Diet soft drinks taste like diet soft drinks. Worse, they prime your taste buds to prefer sweetness, and you want to train them to appreciate subtler flavors. Diet beers will save some calories, mostly because they contain less alcohol. If the lower caloric content encourages you to drink more beer, the breweries will be pleased, since the price is the same as for regular beer.

Desserts and Other Sweets

If desserts are not mostly fat or mostly sugar, they're mostly fat and sugar. True, ice milk has less fat than ice cream, but it can contain more sugar. True, you can buy a pancake syrup with one-third fewer calories, but it's still all sugar. True, you can bake with honey, wheat germ, and soy flour, but the result is still a lot of calories from fat and sugar. There are all sorts of dry biscuits that are sweet without being highly caloric, but you may not find them highly satisfying either.

The real issue when it comes to jams, jellies, syrups, sodas, cookies, cakes, pies, ice creams, and all the rest is the part they play in your eating patterns. Don't forget that two-thirds of the calories in the average American diet are from fat and sugar anyway. So, in a sense, much of what we eat is dessert. If you can restore dessert to its proper nutritional niche, you can end the day with dessert and still eat to win. As you tour the supermarket, reading labels and making choices, consider how many of the things you see are nothing more than desserts masquerading as regular foods. And consider too the most natural desserts of all: fresh fruits.

Artificial Sweeteners

There's no proof that saccharin or other artificial sweeteners are harmful to humans. There's scant evidence that they play a useful part in weight control. Their major drawback is that they will interfere with your efforts to train your taste buds to appreciate the subtler flavors of fruits and lightly sugared sweets. There is nothing subtle about saccharin. If you eat or drink one thing sweetened with it — your coffee or your cereal — fine. But if you get saccharin in your coffee, cereal, soft drinks, *and* desserts, you will be end-running your own efforts to eat to win.

14

Cooking to Win

God sends meat, and the Devil sends cooks.

JOHN TAYLOR (1630)

Kissing don't last; cooking do!

GEORGE MEREDITH
The Ordeal of Richard Feverel

THIS IS NOT A COOKBOOK. If you consider yourself a pretty fair cook already, you won't find anything new or exotic here. What you will find is a series of no-frills, short-order cooking strategies for noncooks that are based on a secret that all cooks share: cooking is far simpler, and more pleasurable, than noncooks think.

To try the suggestions in this chapter, you need only the most basic kitchen gear: a knife for chopping, a spoon for stirring, a mixing bowl, a pot and a pan, a perforated, expandable vegetable steamer, a heavy casserole or a crock pot, and a blender. With only these implements you will be able to follow these simple and nutritious cooking strategies.

1. *Don't cook.* The easiest form of cooking is noncooking. This isn't a recommendation to use the bags you boil or the frozen entrées and desserts you pop into the oven or the toaster. Rather, it's a recommendation to use foods that can be eaten in the state in which they're bought: bread, low-fat milk products, cereals, fruits, and vegetables. The added advantage of raw vegetables is that they have a delicate flavor and have lost none of their nutrients through processing, especially if you store them unwashed, then scrub rather than peel or soak them just prior to serving.

You can add most raw vegetables to almost any salad. By adding a little flaked tuna, garbanzo beans (chick peas), or cottage cheese while you heat a piece of pita bread in the toaster, you make a meal with plenty of protein and carbohydrates and little fat.

Raw vegetables make excellent snacks. When served with no-fat crackers and a low-fat dip, they also make a meal. Low-fat dips, dressings, and sauces can be made with any dried soup or salad-dressing mix. In making onion dip, for example, substitute cottage cheese or yogurt for sour cream. In preparing creamy, ranch-type dressings, use buttermilk instead of oil or mayonnaise. In making traditional oil-and-vinegar dressings, use tomato juice or puree. Check out the low-fat dressings that are available in supermarkets. The versions you make from scratch, however, will taste fresher and contain less salt. Try making a cold gazpacho-type soup in the blender, using any combination of tomatoes, cucumbers, squash, green peppers, onions, garlic, and parsley. Thin it with tomato juice for a soup; thicken it with tomato paste for a dip; spice it with chilis, other red peppers, or hot sauce.

Raw fruits are equally flexible for the noncook. Eating them as they are is easiest. But you can make fruit shakes by pureeing your favorite fruit in the blender along with skim milk and/or seltzer, plus a flavoring like vanilla extract or cinnamon. Or you can dissolve a package of plain gelatin in hot water, add it to the blender, pour the mixture into a bowl or cups, and refrigerate it to make fruit gelatin. Another trick is to puree one fruit — say, strawberries — and pour the puree over another fruit, say, bananas. In moments of extravagance, add a level teaspoon of sugar per serving.

2. *Boil water.* To prepare rice, potato, and pasta dishes, all you have to do is boil water, cook, drain, and top them with a low-fat dressing. (Rinsing cooked pasta under running water washes off the surface starch that makes it sticky.) You can top pasta with a bottled sauce, or you can make your own.

The simplest sauce is a can of tomatoes or tomato puree, which may be thickened with tomato paste and flavored with chopped onions, garlic, mushrooms, green peppers, or herbs. Bring the ingredients to a boil; then simmer gently while the pasta is cooking. You can make this sauce by the quart and store it in the refrigerator. You can add any vegetable to the sauce while it's simmering. You can cook the chopped vegetables with a little chopped or ground meat as it browns; just be sure to pour off the fat before adding the meat and vegetables to the sauce.

3. *Steam.* Steaming vegetables is a superior way to retain flavor and nutrients. It takes only a little water. If you want to reclaim the vitamins that do leach into the water, make a sauce with the water by adding a little nonfat dry milk or evaporated milk. Bite-size pieces of chicken and seafood can also be steamed right along with the vegetables. They take a minute or two longer; so put them into the steamer first. Then layer on the vegetables. Serve with bread, or pour over rice or noodles.

4. *Poach.* You can simmer larger pieces of fish and chicken, along with chopped vegetables and seasonings, in water or broth. Add cooked rice or pasta, and you'll have a one-bowl main dish that's something between a stew and a soup.

5. *Puree.* You can make vegetable soup simply by simmering vegetables in broth. You can then puree the soup in a blender. It's as good cold as it is hot. You can also blend in nonfat dry milk, or evaporated milk, buttermilk, or yogurt for a hot or cold, creamy soup. Eat it with hot, fresh bread, or stir in cooked rice or noodles, and you'll have a meal.

6. *Slow-cook.* Slow-cooking enables noncooks with busy schedules to come home to a nutritious hot meal. In the morning, put meat, water, or broth, and seasonings in a crock pot or casserole, and turn the crock pot on, or set the casserole in a low-temperature oven (275–300 degrees). Add vegetables when you get home, and eat the results a little later.

7. *Fast-cook.* Stir-frying — cooking small pieces of meat and vegetables in a small amount of hot oil — was developed in the Far East, where cooking fuels have long been in short supply. It actually takes longer to chop the foods than it does to cook them. Stir-frying is easy in a wok, and not much harder in a pan.

8. *Barbecue.* Grilling and charcoal-broiling are traditionally the provinces of noncooks. Ironically, these methods require more preparation time and attention than any of the forms of cooking mentioned above. Their main nutritional drawback is the understandable urge they create to cook huge hamburgers and slabs of meat. But they are tasty ways to cook potatoes, chicken, fish, and shishkebab.

9. *Change the recipe.* There's almost no recipe that calls for sugar, butter, margarine, or shortening that can't be made with less (and probably was a century ago). If you experiment, you'll find that you

can usually cut the fat by a third and the sugar by a half in the things you bake or broil. You can usually omit the salt entirely and compensate by using other flavorings. (It'll take a little experimenting to find out how far you can go with your favorite recipes before they stop being your favorites.) Extend ground meats with bread crumbs, unsweetened cereals, or rice.

A Week of Winning

In *The "Average American" Book,* Barry Tarshis notes that "Americans are essentially conservative when it comes to food preferences, and as most food specialists estimate, no more than 10 percent of the population has anything approaching an adventurous palate." This fact of life is reflected in the eating strategies and menu ideas below. The only foods that you might consider even slightly exotic are tofu (the bland, highly nutritious curd made from soybeans), pita bread, and yogurt. In each instance, there are numerous options that are nutritious and entirely ordinary.

Breakfast

Mom is right. You need a good breakfast. When you get up in the morning, your body's reserves of protein and carbohydrates are at their lowest and must be replenished. Studies have revealed that people who eat breakfast perform better, both physically and mentally. They have greater alertness, faster reaction times, and less muscular fatigue. They have fewer problems with their weight. They even live longer. So don't skip breakfast.

A good breakfast isn't a traditional high-fat, bacon-and-eggs, toast-and-butter breakfast. Nor is it a commercial breakfast-drink mix that adds fat and sugar to milk. An Eat-to-Win breakfast is high in complex carbohydrates, low in sugar, moderate in protein, and low in fat. It will sit lightly on your stomach, and it will get out of your stomach and into your system quickly. Breakfast is also the traditional time to get your daily dose of vitamin C, usually from orange juice or half a grapefruit.

An Eat-to-Win Instant Breakfast

There is no commercial liquid meal, instant breakfast, or milk shake that doesn't contain too much fat and sugar. But you can make one that doesn't have these drawbacks. Although it may sound a bit peculiar, satisfaction is guaranteed.

Cook a big batch of Instant Cream of Wheat, following package directions but using water and no salt. This will take five minutes. Cool the cereal and store it in the refrigerator. The next morning, put two or more heaping spoonfuls of the cereal into a blender, along with a glass of skim milk and any flavoring you want: vanilla extract, cinnamon, orange-juice concentrate, any ripe fruit. The thickness can be varied to suit your preference. The flavoring provides taste, as does the milk, which also provides protein. The cereal adds body, no taste, and abundant complex carbohydrates.

Menu Ideas

1. Any low-sugar, whole-grain cereal with skim milk. Juice. Tea or coffee (with skim milk).

2. Whole-wheat toast with low-fat cottage cheese. Half a grapefruit. Tea or coffee.

3. Pita bread stuffed with one slice of reduced-fat American cheese and warmed in toaster or oven. Juice. Tea or coffee.

4. An English muffin with mock marmalade (yogurt cheese with a spoonful of orange-juice concentrate). Tea or coffee.

5. Leftover rice with skim milk, sliced banana, and cinnamon. Juice. Tea or coffee.

6. A poached egg on whole-wheat bread. Juice. Tea or coffee.

7. Eat-to-Win instant breakfast.

Lunch

Lunch, as well as breakfast, should be a low-fat meal. But coming up with a low-fat lunch takes a little more effort, especially if you're out of the house. The formula, however, is almost the same as for breakfast. It substitutes vegetables for the citrus fruit, and it features bread, rice, pasta, crackers, or potatoes. It also includes a small amount of animal protein in the form of fish, meat, or dairy food, or a vegetable protein like peanut butter or beans.

Menu Ideas

1. A grilled cheese and tomato sandwich (made with low-fat American cheese and without extra oil or butter) garnished with raw vegetables.

2. A salad of raw vegetables, and garbanzo or other beans or a sprinkling of tuna, with low-fat dressing. Warmed pita bread.

3. A *plain* fast-food hamburger. A piece of fruit.

4. Homemade vegetable soup, creamed with low-fat milk or buttermilk. Noodles or a roll.

5. A peanut butter and banana sandwich made with whole-wheat bread.

6. Plain yogurt with fresh fruit, served over leftover rice and dusted with cinnamon.

7. Pita bread stuffed with chopped vegetables and cottage or farmer's cheese.

Beverage: Tea or coffee (with skim milk), fruit or vegetable juice, broth, water, or fresh fruit shake.

Dinner

The basic formula is the same for dinner: a large serving of a high-carbohydrate food, a moderate serving of a high-protein food, and vegetables. This is the meal where you can use extra fat if you have eaten little during the day, or cut back on fat if you've exceeded the amount you feel you should eat. This is also the traditional time to have meat.

Menu Ideas

1. Vegetable soup. Baked chicken. Noodles.

2. Meat loaf (extended with a grain). Steamed vegetables or salad with raw vegetables and low-fat dressing.

3. Pork-and-beans. Fresh bread. Salad with raw vegetables and low-fat dressing.

4. Veal stew with vegetables and potatoes. Bread.

5. Split pea soup with ham. Pita bread. Salad with raw vegetables and low-fat dressing.

6. Steamed fish and vegetables over rice, or fish and vegetables simmered in chicken stock with tofu cubes.

7. Pasta with clams and vegetables (steamed over clam broth), or with tomato sauce, vegetables, and Parmesan, or with meat sauce. Salad with raw vegetables and low-fat dressing.

The Pregame Meal

No one meal is ideal for everyone before exercising or competing. In fact, psychological satisfactions can be more important than optimal nutritional standards before the big game. If your overall eating patterns are sound, the contents of your pregame meal won't matter much. Eat what is comforting and familiar. If certain foods are nutritionally unbalanced but psychologically important, stay with them. Otherwise, consider the following guidelines and findings.

1. *Timing.* Playing on an empty stomach will help avoid stomach upset. Generally, this means eating no later than two to three hours before the event. Certain kinds of meals and individual differences, however, can shorten this time considerably. But there's no evidence that eating closer to starting time improves performance.

2. *Liquid or solid.* Studies of pregame meals have shown no performance advantage from either liquid or solid meals. In one study, however, a 900-calorie liquid meal as late as thirty minutes prior to exercise cleared the stomach and had no detrimental effects.

3. *High in complex carbohydrates.* Meals that are high in complex carbohydrates clear the stomach and are digested quickly. And they provide the ideal fuel for heavy exercise.

4. *Low in sugar.* Taking in refined sugar prior to competition primes the body to burn glycogen faster.

5. *Low in fat.* High-fat meals stay in the stomach longest and take the longest to be digested.

6. *High in fluids.* During the game, water is the single most important nutrient. Before the game, avoid liquids such as alcohol, which will dehydrate, reduce heat tolerance, and interfere with judgment. Drink plenty of water, the optimal athletic fluid.

Beverage: Tea or coffee (with skim milk), sparkling water, fruit juice, or wine or beer in moderation.

Dessert: Fruit gelatin, fruit puree over fruit, or yogurt with fruit.

Treats

Anywhere along the way, you can add to or alter these sample menus with a treat that is high in fat or sugar: commercial fruit yogurt, French fries, half-and-half on fruits, a few cookies, ice

---

If You Shop and Cook for Others

People who are lucky enough to have a parent, spouse, or significant other to shop and cook for them ought to be grateful for whatever they get. In the real world, however, they may resist and resent your efforts to change the way you eat if it affects the way they eat. Some people — bless them — will eat whatever is put in front of them. Others will turn up their noses at the slightest change. You can try to share your Eat-to-Win goals. You can make substitutions that no one will resent because no one will notice (skim milk they'll notice, 1 percent–fat milk they won't). You can shop alone, stop bringing things home that you don't want anyone to eat, and see what develops. If the cry goes up for junk-food snacks, have an alternative ready, but don't palm it off as a just-as-good-as substitute. If the cry continues, tell them to shop for what they want. Point out that, since it's your job to make sure they eat well, there are things you will do and things you won't do. Since we're talking strategy, however, follow this basic rule: never fight over food. In fights over food, the real issue is not a nutritional one. Like fights over sex and money, fights over food usually cover power struggles — you're angry that you can't have it your way — or dented self-esteem — you're hurt that your efforts as caretaker aren't better appreciated. Back off. Bide your time. Remember, *you* do the shopping and cooking.

---

cream, oil-based salad dressing, a pat of butter on vegetables. Treat yourself well, but keep an eye on your overall pattern.

Snacks

Fruits: Fresh or dried fruit; fruit shake (using nonfat dry milk and seltzer, or the recipe for the Eat-to-Win instant breakfast); fruit juice extended with seltzer or water; chopped or pureed fresh fruit in plain gelatin.

Vegetables: Any raw vegetable, plain or with low-fat dip, mustard, or horseradish.

Grain Products: Any no-fat cracker, chip, or pretzel, plain or with a low-fat dip.

Trail Mix: Dried fruit combined with unsalted nuts or soy nuts, and a low-sugar, bite-size cereal.

If Someone Shops and Cooks for You

If you're lucky enough to have a parent, spouse, or significant other to shop and cook for you, count your blessings first. Then realize that they may not feel the same need to eat to win as you do. Enlisting their help requires tact. Remember, you're getting a free ride as it is; and the people who are shopping and cooking are doing what they think is best. You should discuss the reasons why you want to make changes. They may not understand or agree, but they will usually help if they don't feel as if they're under attack. Keep in mind that you can't change without a positive motivation and that they won't help unless they have one too. They will probably buy foods that you can eat as they are, especially if they're cheaper. But don't expect people to change the way they feed themselves or the rest of the household. Instead, plan to exercise extra willpower at the table: ask for a smaller serving of meat and more fillers and vegetables; skip the sauces; and have a smaller serving of dessert. Since we're talking strategy, follow this basic rule: never fight over food. In fights over food, the real issue is not a nutritional one. Like fights over sex and money, fights over food usually cover a power struggle — you're angry that you can't have it your way — or dented self-esteem — you're hurt that they aren't more cooperative. Back off. Concentrate on behavior, not words. Your chance to influence the people who shop and cook for you is best when you set the right example.

15

Out of the House and On the Road

Proportion of meals eaten out:
1. *Weekday lunches* — 37 percent
2. *Weekday dinners* — 17 percent
3. *Weekend breakfasts* — 15 percent
4. *Weekend lunches* — 28 percent
5. *Weekend dinners* — 32 percent

1978 Newspaper Advertising Bureau Survey

WHETHER IT'S BECAUSE we're at school or at work, on vacation or on the competitive circuit, or just bored with cooking, we end up eating a third of our meals away from our homes. This makes it harder to eat to win, because we can't control the menu or the way the food is prepared. *We're* the customers, however, and there are a lot of decisions we can make that will drastically reduce our consumption of fat and sugar.

Fast-Food Restaurants. When you eat out, you most often head for a fast-food restaurant if you're like most Americans. The real problem with burger, chicken, pizza, and fish places is not that the food lacks nutrients. Almost any entrée will meet half or more of your RDA for protein, for example. The main problem is that too many calories in these foods are from fat and too few from complex carbohydrates. It's not all "their" fault. Some chains have experimented with salad bars, and the customers have studiously ignored them. This leaves you with main dishes and fries that are over 50 percent fat and with drinks and desserts that get almost all their calories from fat and sugar.

The only answer is to hold back. Order the most basic entrée — a hamburger without the cheese or special sauce, a chicken breast, a slice of pizza, fish sticks — and leave it at that. Order milk to drink. Or fruit *juice,* if there's a breakfast menu. Or water. Skip the soft drinks and shakes. At this point, you may be wondering why go in at all. It's for a meal that's fast, familiar, and cheap. Only if you can prevent yourself from going in too often should you order the fries and the shake. Otherwise, settle for an entrée, and invest the money you save in a piece of fruit.

Other Restaurants. Even inexpensive diners and coffee shops offer enough variety to allow you to put together decent ·meals. You don't have to order the bacon-and-egg breakfast. Have some shredded wheat or All-Bran with a banana. For lunch or dinner, you might not find a salad on the menu, but you can usually get a side order of lettuce and tomato. Order two "sides." If you aren't allowed to make substitutions, order à la carte if you must; reduce your tip accordingly. If almost everything is deep-fried or buried under a sauce, try for a baked potato, a can of tuna, a fruit salad, extra bread, or a diet platter. Ironically, diet platters have the same percentage of fat as a regular meal, but they are lower in calories. If none of these ploys work, do the best you can with what is available, and compensate at the next meal. Remember, no one meal will ever unhinge your basic eating patterns. So, if you're at a restaurant that has the best ribs, pâté de fois gras, or baked Alaska in town, order and enjoy.

Delicatessens. A decent deli is actually a minisupermarket. It'll make any sandwich you want — hold the mayo; have meat *or* cheese — and it'll usually have fresh fruits or fruit salads as well as vegetable salads. Just skip the egg salad made with mayonnaise, the processed meats, and the alluring desserts, and you'll walk out a winner.

Cafeterias. No one likes institutional food. Even professional athletes complain about the fare at training camps. But you can usually make choices. If the vegetables have been cooked into total submission, double up on the fresh salad. Take the fruit instead of the fruit gelatin. Who says that you have to have both the mystery meat and the creamed-potato surprise? If you don't put a food on your tray, you won't put it in your mouth.

Room Service. These days, room service offers a shorter menu than it used to; the hours of service have been curtailed; and the waiting time can seem eternal. Still, you ought to be able to order a sandwich, a continental breakfast with a large glass of orange juice, or perhaps a chef's salad or fruit salad. In fact, the more basic the order, the more likely you are to enjoy it when it finally arrives.

Social Gatherings. Parties and other group festivities invite overconsumption of food and drink. If your life is a continual party, however, you have to watch what you eat and drink. Even if the host or hostess has gone to considerable trouble to lay out an overcaloric spread for everyone, there may be valid reasons to pass it up — for example, if you are a vegetarian or have diabetes, hypertension, heart disease, or an allergy *and* if you've called in advance to pass on this information. Otherwise, it's poor manners even if it's good nutrition. Eat small portions, avoid the sauces, compliment the chef, and compensate at your next meal.

Airplanes. Although they don't make a big point of it, most airlines offer vegetarian meals and diet plates. These have to be ordered in advance, but they usually have fewer calories, less fat, and more taste than the regular food.

Brown Bags. One way to ensure finding the foods you like when you're out of the house or on the road is to take them along. A bag need contain only bread, a little meat or cheese, a few carrot sticks, and some dried or fresh fruit or fruit juice to provide a well-rounded meal. For longer trips, you can pack dried foods: your favorite breakfast cereal, nonfat dry milk, dried fruit or trail mix, instant coffee, bouillon cubes. If you're tempted to toss in a few "high-protein" bars or powdered protein supplements, read the labels. They're mostly sugar and fat. Have a bowl of cereal instead.

* * *

Eating out, especially if it's a regular part of your life, takes discipline if you're going to eat to win, because you will be surrounded by people enjoying foods that you "shouldn't" have. However, even if you succumb to temptation, you always have the option to compensate at your next meal. If you find that eating out upsets — or becomes — the basic pattern, then overcompensate with a day or two of the Intensive Training diet.

16

Carbohydrate Loading

No rule is so general that it admits not some exception.

JOHN BURTON (1577–1640)

As long as fuel supply is one of the factors contributing to exhaustion, you're always going to be able to manipulate diet in hopes of extracting a better performance. We're now studying the effects of vitamins, minerals, and various food sources on glycogen depletion. Training methods are pretty well understood. Nutrition is the virgin field.

DAVID COSTILL
in *Runner's World*

HUMANS ARE BORN CURIOUS, and given what is still not known about nutrition, the future should excite our curiosity. But the future — and the excitement — should be placed in the context of what *is* known about nutrition and performance. Optimal nutrition is the same for all athletes. What benefits the distance runner will benefit the bodybuilder. The reason is simple: all athletes want energy, and optimal nutrition supplies that energy to all athletes. The exceptions to this rule are few and apply to a few athletes, specifically, elite endurance athletes.

Most experts say it takes even the most promising and dedicated athletes three to five years of serious training to near their full potential. If you are still striving to reach this goal, you'll do best to stick to the basics of optimal nutrition. When you do, you can train for increased strength and stamina in complete confidence that nutrition is doing essentially all it can to improve your performance.

Understandably, however, endurance athletes at the top levels of competition are willing to experiment with any nutritional manipulation that may afford them a competitive edge. The only such manipulation that is known to be effective is carbohydrate loading, and even top-ranked athletes are divided on its usefulness.

If you are considering this diet, review the information on carbohydrates, energy, and loading in chapter 6. Remember too that you may have to experiment with this diet to obtain the best results. Avoiding carbohydrates for three days may cause an unacceptable loss of energy. Loading carbohydrates for three days may cause muscle soreness and stiffness. You may not like the disruption in your training schedule. By skipping the low-carbohydrate phase altogether, you will then be following the high-carbohydrate regimen that is the basis of the Eat-to-Win plan. In doing so, you will receive most of the benefits of strict loading, with none of the disadvantages. Finally, most experts recommend limiting strict carbohydrate loading to no more than once every six weeks.

Day 1. Your first step is a long, hard workout designed to deplete muscle glycogen. Go past whatever version of the wall you experience by ten to twenty minutes to ensure complete glycogen depletion. For the rest of the day, avoid all high-carbohydrate foods, such as grain products, potatoes, beans, sugar, and fruits, and eat meat, fish, milk and dairy products, low-calorie salads and vegetables with regular, high-fat dressings.

Days 2 and 3. Have a light workout, or rest. Continue your low-carbohydrate, high-protein, high-fat regimen. This diet will be starving your muscles of glycogen. It might also cause you to lose weight through copious urination. So be sure to drink plenty of fluids. Rather than getting your few carbohydrates from an occasional piece of bread, get them from fresh fruits. You need the electrolytes.

Day 4. Stay on the low-carbohydrate diet until after a hard workout of moderate length to guarantee total glycogen depletion. Following that, you are ready to commence carbohydrate loading. Switch to high-carbohydrate foods, such as grains and grain products, potatoes, beans, sugar, and fruits, and limit your use of high-fat meats, dairy products, salad dressings, and so forth.

Days 5 and 6. Have a light to moderate workout (remember, you're storing glycogen), and continue your high-carbohydrate diet.

Day 7. This is the day you compete. Continue your carbohydrate loading, or have your favorite pregame meal.

*　*　*

Most of us, of course, are not training to be champions, except in our own eyes. We want to do our personal best. It's tempting to try anything that works for some top-notch endurance athletes. But will we benefit? Caffeine, for example, has a slight but significant ability to slow glycogen depletion (see chapter 11). But as Dr. David Costill, the physiologist who made this discovery, told *The Runner*, "I play it down now because it's a drug, and I don't want anyone to feel they have to pop a pill in order to turn in a good performance." Is Costill merely being moralistic — or practical-minded? In fact, too many athletes will try any special substance or diet, in ignorance or at the expense of sound eating habits. The basics, of course, whether in nutrition or in sports, are not especially exciting. They're just essential. What athletes looking for a shortcut need to know is what Dr. Costill and other diet–performance experts will tell them: no special substance or diet — and, in all probability, no future nutritional discovery — offers athletes the performance benefits of optimal nutrition.

17

Losing Weight to Win

Ascribing overweight to overeating is hardly more illuminating than ascribing alcoholism to over-drinking.

JEAN MAYER

Like liberty, the price of leanness is eternal vigilance.

THEODORE VAN ITALLIE

Obesity is the most widespread nutritional disorder in this country. It is a psychological burden and a serious health hazard.

JOSÉ LUIS BARBOSA-SALDIVAR
Columbia University College
of Physicians and Surgeons

EXCESS FAT IS the visible evidence of overfueling, and just about everyone knows that the solution to this condition is to eat less, burn more fuel, or both. What just about everyone who loses weight — nine out of ten, in fact — also knows is that lost weight inevitably returns. If you have ever experienced what nutritionist Jean Mayer calls "the rhythm method of girth control," your first step in losing weight to win is to understand the causes of obesity. You will then have the all-important theoretical foundation that will enable you to apply the practical principles of permanent weight loss.

The Causes of Obesity

The Social Dimension. Obesity is much more common today than it was a century ago. Lifestyles and eating patterns have changed dramatically. We live in a society that promotes inactivity via energy-saving technology. Only the most active athletes are as active as most people were a century ago. True, our caloric intake has declined, but our activity levels have declined even more.

The Genetic Dimension. We're all born with an ability to conserve energy and store it as fat. Those who are better at doing this have a survival advantage in feast-or-famine conditions. But in a society like ours, where the food supply is predictable and abundant, many of us are at a disadvantage when it comes to losing weight and keeping it off.

The Family Dimension. If one parent is fat, an offspring has a 40 percent chance of being fat. If both are fat, the chances increase to at least 80 percent. A genetic factor is almost certainly at work here, in unhappy combination with family eating habits. As a result, a lot of people are condemned to struggle with obesity long before they ever make a single conscious decision about what they eat. Eating patterns are learned from parents, and if parents are overweight, they almost certainly overfeed their children. In extreme cases, the result of this feeding behavior is an inability to interpret the basic physical signs of hunger and fullness accurately. This problem continues until eating patterns have been permanently changed. It *is* possible to get back in touch with the "appestat." Yet even when the motivation for change is strong and positive, the earliest habits are the hardest to modify.

The Biochemical Dimension. Each of us has billions of fat cells. The exact number is determined largely during the third trimester of pregnancy and in infancy. (Adolescents who gain a great deal of weight also add fat cells, and so do adults, though to a lesser extent. But most of the additional fat is deposited in fat cells that already exist.) By the time we're ready for school, we have practically all the fat cells we're going to have, and although we can reduce their size, we cannot reduce their number. Adults who were fat babies may have 80–120 billion fat cells, rather than the typical 30–40 billion. Like tiny balloons that occupy space even when deflated, these excess fat cells make it that much harder for them to look and stay thin. Each fat cell may contain less fat than the average, but burdened with so many fat cells, these people *look* and *are* fatter. The training challenge they face is to shrink their fat cells to a smaller than normal size and keep them that way. It's an unfortunate fact of life that fat cells resist attempts to shrink them and, once shrunk, easily reinflate to normal size.

The biochemistry of fat is complex and imperfectly understood. Overweight people may be *under*supplied with brown fat, the beneficial kind of fat that helps burn excess calories rather than store them. They definitely have a subtly different blood chemistry than people of average weight. (The implications of this difference are now under investigation.) And they definitely need fewer calories than more muscular people of the same weight, because fat burns fuel more slowly than muscle does. The result of all these differences is something that all overweight people must accept: they can gain or regain weight on a diet whose caloric content would have no effect, or even a negative effect, on the weight of other people.

The Psychological Dimension. There is tremendous prejudice against fat people in our society. This prejudice equates overweight with unattractiveness, lack of willpower, and low self-esteem. As a result, many fat people are burdened with anger, guilt, and self-consciousness, all of which interfere with their happiness and their attempts to lose weight. Like any other minority, fat people must learn that what makes them different does not make them inferior. They might be able to lose a certain amount of weight because they feel bad about their size, but they will be able to maintain that loss only if they feel good about themselves.

Training Strategies for Losing Weight

Understanding the causes of obesity can provide a solid, scientific foundation for your efforts to lose weight and maintain that loss. Still, although you can't play the game until you know the ground rules, you won't be any good at the game unless you practice. Reaching your desired weight, and then staying there, require the same kind of dedicated training you devote to your sport — and can benefit from the same kind of practical training strategies.

Be Realistic. Obesity has its drawbacks on and off playing fields. But crash-dieting, aside from the entirely predictable return of lost weight, is a lot harder on your health and energy than is maintaining a weight that is higher than your ideal. You may be tempted by reports of easy, effortless ways to lose weight, which are usually accompanied by an "if only" pitch for some product or plan. Resist the temptation to try them. The more overweight you are and the longer you have been overweight, the more work it will take to reach and maintain your desired weight and the less you will ever be able to eat like most other people. So start with a realistic goal. Make sure you aren't exaggerating the effects that weighing less will have. You *can* look, feel, and perform better. But nutrition isn't magic, and changing your weight won't transform your life. Give the matter some hard thought, and pick a weight that represents a realistic training challenge. Now you're off and running.

Maintain a Positive Attitude. A positive motivation for change is the most powerful weapon in the battle of the bulge, and in the effort to improve eating patterns. Lose weight to perform better, feel better, look better. First and foremost, do it for yourself. Positive thinking means taking the responsibility for your weight. Whatever the reasons, you are the one who gained the weight, and only you can take it off. Positive thinking means being goal-oriented. Guilt, blame, and anger are negative feelings. They will point you backward, toward the problem, when you should be looking ahead, toward the solution. Positive thinking means making choices and changes. If you can learn the basic difference between self-enhancement and self-denial, you will have a much better chance of reaching and maintaining your desired weight.

Maintain Perspective. If you pin all your hopes on reaching a goal — losing a certain amount of weight by a certain time, making the team, coming in first — you may end up missing out on a lot of satisfaction. What makes victory sweetest, and defeat most tolerable, is knowing that you worked hard, did your best, and kept faith with yourself. When winning the big game or reaching a certain weight becomes all-important, you lose perspective. When winning is everything, you have only one chance for satisfaction. When getting there is at least half the fun, your chances increase proportionally. The most satisfying benefits of eating right and playing well go far beyond the immediate moment. They are life-long.

Focus on Patterns. The biggest problem most people have with nutrition is that they focus on specifics — how much protein, how many vitamins, or how many calories to take in — without considering the big picture. No one thing you do to improve your performance, your health, or your weight, is nearly as important as the overall thrust of your training. Every change you make in your training should be considered in the context of your basic training patterns. Taking vitamins, for example, is meaningless when your eating patterns are unbalanced, and unnecessary when they aren't.

Concentrating on your eating patterns will also help you deal with the Achilles' heel of most dieters: cheating. To begin with, the connotations of the word are negative. We've been taught that cheating is sinful, unethical, and unsporting. And we believe that cheaters never prosper, because, at the very least, they're condemned to be themselves. So banish the word from your nutritional vocabulary. Substitute *breaking training* or, in the spirit of positive thinking, *easing up* or *changing pace.*

Whatever term you prefer, taking a training break is a problem only when it becomes the pattern. If you skip too many practices, then skipping, not practicing, will be your pattern, and you'll get cut from the team. The same applies to your eating habits. Easing up or taking a break from time to time is, at worst, irrelevant and may even be beneficial. It's an antidote for overtraining and an outlet for boredom, rebelliousness, and anxiety. The result: you return to your training with renewed energy and commitment.

Be Patient. The secret of scientific training is progressive training. You know what happens when you push too hard and go too far too fast. This overtraining invariably sets you back. The same principle applies when you're dieting. Losing weight too quickly is counterproductive. It won't produce the results you want, and it'll undermine the motivation you need to keep going.

Losing weight fast requires a drastic reduction in caloric intake. Whether you crash-diet by going on any of the endless fad diets or diet drugs, a diet that is ultralow in calories is, by definition, nutritionally unbalanced. Some are worse than others. High-protein diets — the ones that sell like crazy — restrict the intake of the carbohydrates that are the cornerstone of a high-energy diet. The

---

A Few Words on Calories

Calories count, but counting calories is an exercise in futility and frustration. Worse, it promotes nutritional tunnel vision. The result: you focus on a food and ignore an eating pattern.

The moment you find yourself concerned about calories, review your eating pattern of the preceding week or so. Ask yourself the following questions: Did I eat too much? too often? Did I feel stuffed? Did I get too much added fat in the form of overprocessed convenience foods? fast foods? fried foods? high-fat milk and meat products? sauces? dips? chips? desserts? Did I take in too much added sugar from the sugar bowl? from overprocessed foods? from candy? from cakes, pies, cookies, or other rich desserts? Did I drink too much alcohol? Did I get too little fiber from whole-grain products? from fresh fruits and vegetables?

If you answered yes to any of these questions, make those issues your training goals. Your caloric intake will then take care of itself. If you answered no to all of the questions, your eating patterns are fine. You should just stop worrying about calories altogether, or reduce your portions slightly and/or increase your physical activity to lose weight.

---

evidence is clear that in the long run, these diets are less effective than balanced diets with the same number of calories. But because they cause rapid water loss, they *seem* more effective and so remain popular with uninformed dieters.

No crash diet, however, addresses the central issue: developing the lifelong, day-in, day-out eating patterns that you will need to maintain your energy, health, and weight. Crash diets are also ineffective because they trigger survival mechanisms that cause your body to conserve its fat stores more efficiently. You'll notice the difference in your energy level. In fact, you cannot lose more than two pounds a week through diet alone *without compromising your strength and stamina.* For any athlete, this is the most immediate drawback of crash-dieting.

The Next Step

These training strategies, together with an understanding of the causes of obesity, give you a context in which to place your weight-loss efforts. Now you need a specific diet plan. Choose either of the Eat-to-Win plans recommended for other athletes. Your nutritional needs are the same as theirs. True, you will have to work harder to reach your special nutritional goals. But that will make your victory all the sweeter.

Index